ECHOES FROM THE PAST

TRIUMPH OF A PRAIRIE SPIRIT

MARY VICTORIA MIDDLETON DEBOON

Groundswell Publishing
Toronto

Groundswell Publishing
168 Drayton Ave.
Toronto, Ontario
M4C 3M2

Quotes from Francis E. Burn's book, *True Pioneer Stories*, Mike Byneshewsky's photograph
of Carmangay, and Lyseng Studio's photo (back cover) are used with permission.

Library and Archives Canada Cataloguing in Publication

deBoon, Mary Victoria Middleton, 1928-
Echoes from the past : Triumph of a prairie spirit / Mary Victoria Middleton deBoon.

ISBN 0-9738674-0-X

1. deBoon, Mary Victoria Middleton, 1928-. 2. Single mothers—Alberta—Biography.
3. Alberta—Biography. 4. Alberta—History, Local.
I. Title.

FC3675.1.D42A3 2005   971.23'304'092
C2005-904332-6

Printed and bound in Canada

Developmental editing: Ellen Long
Layout and design: Ellie Robinson
Copy editing: Susan Lawrence and Eve Goldberg

Ordering Information
Orders by individulas, Canadian trade bookstores, wholesalers, organizations or
educational institutions: Please contact Groundswell Publishing,
168 Drayton Ave., Toronto, Ontario, M4C 3M2; phone toll free,
 1-866-252-2463; or email, groundswellpublishing@bellnet.ca.
This book may be purchased in bulk for educational or promotional use.

Groundswell Publishing provides book coaching, editing, design and printing of books for individuals and
organizations. For more information, contact the publisher.

For my family, with love

Prairie Grain Elevators in Carmangay, Alberta

Photo by © Mike Byneshewsky

Contents

Introduction & Acknowledgments

I wrote this book as a legacy for my children and my children's children. I started it when I was about 50 years of age. At that time, I wrote about the first ten years of my life because there was a family reunion coming up and I wanted to have some history written down for it. I didn't write anything more for many years and then, when I was close to 70, I wrote the rest of my story. As well as memory serves, I have put into words the many events that have molded me into the person I am today. I would like to thank my daughter Ellen Long for all of her help in putting this book together.

Mary Middleton deBoon
Camrose, Alberta
July 2005

Echoes from the Past: Triumph of a Prairie Spirit was originally printed in small numbers in 1999 for our extended family. The book got passed from hand to hand and before long, an avalanche of people from outside our family were phoning, writing or visiting to find out how they could buy copies for themselves or their family members. In addition to being "gripped" and "inspired," they saw the book as a compelling model for how to document their own life stories or family histories. Sadly, we had only printed 60 copies and none were for sale. And so, in celebration of Alberta's centennial year, and in answer to the many requests we received, we are printing a second edition of the book for individuals, museum archives, local historical societies and libraries.

I am deeply honoured to have helped my mother put this book together. In my late teens, I remember seeing her hunched over the kitchen table writing about the early years of her life. Twenty years later, when I was learning the publishing trade, I surprised her with a book cover I had designed with her name on it and asked if she would complete her story. After a short bout of anxiety about "spelling, grammar and punctuation," her writing poured out in a rural Prairie voice, straight from the heart. Thanks to her willingness to talk about both the good times and the bad, Mary's indomitable strength of character and irrepressible sense of humour were shining through on every page like a sturdy wildflower in a drought-stricken wheat field. Mary's story shows how people of the Prairies had to survive-to blossom (or not)-wherever they happened to be planted.

Many, including Mary herself, were amazed that someone who had never done much writing could suddenly produce a book-length manuscript that was so enjoyable to read. But like many rural Prairie people, she tells a good story and she has dozens of them, increasingly polished in the telling. In fact, many of her life challenges were weathered with grace, thanks in part, to the promise of "a good story" coming out of the experiences. Mary has a talent for story-telling as she has for painting. When she was close to 60 years of age, she picked up a paintbrush for the first time and immediately created beautiful works of art. This seemed almost miraculous in the absence of formal training or at least an extended period of practice. So, too, with her writing. There it was.

Mary's life story spans more than 70 years. It begins with the world on the brink of the Great Depression and ends with the world on the cusp of a new century. Interspersed with her story, are colourful and often poignant quotes from her five children-Cathy, age 47; Linda, 45; Ida, 41; Ellen, 38; and David, 33-along with her sisters, her brother, a step-son, grandchildren, schoolteachers, friends, boarders, workmates, customers, and neighbours. These quotes, a surprise for Mary, were included to add texture to the rich stories she tells.

I would like to thank the many people who helped put this book together, including my sisters and brother who sent pictures on a moment's notice and endured relentless phone calls for background information, Susan Lawrence for her encouragement and editing skills, and Ellie Robinson for a beautiful job on layout and design. Thanks also to those who heartened us to republish the book for a larger audience. I owe a special debt of gratitude to my partner Eve for her extensive practical help and her patient heart during the marathon that gave birth to this book.

Ellen Long
Groundswell Publishing
Toronto, Ontario
July 2005

Life is harsh sometimes, but with perseverance and faith that there is a brighter tomorrow, we can pull through. And of course everything has a funny side.

Mary Middleton deBoon

We all have stories to tell, stories that provide wisdom about the journey of life. What more have we to give one another than our truth about our human adventure as honestly and as openly as we know how?

Saul Rubin

1

Homestead Beginnings: Carmangay — 1928 to 1947

On June 3, 1928 a 10-pound baby girl was born to Thomas and Ellen Middleton on a homestead west of Carmangay. They named her Mary Victoria Middleton — Mary, after Jesus' mother, and Victoria, after the Queen of England. The baby was me! My place of birth was in a farm home by Little Bow River. At 5:00 a.m., my brother, Walter, and my three sisters, Thelma, Francis and Edna, had to get out of their warm beds and go walking by the river in their bare feet. The doctor and the midwife from town didn't make it on time. Luckily, my grandmother, who was a midwife, was visiting from England and she delivered me. The town midwife, a Scottish nurse, arrived at 5:30 a.m. and brought me downstairs wrapped in a newspaper. My dad, standing at the bottom of the stairs, said, "Shall I take that out to the garbage?"

"Oh nay," the nurse exclaimed in her thick Scottish brogue, "Tis the wee bairn!" So was my entrance into this harsh world, and after receiving my first bath in front of the coal and wood stove, life began for me.

My Parents

Almost a century ago, my immediate family had its beginnings in the marriage of Thomas Middleton and Ellen Scott on June 29, 1910. They were married at St. Augustine's church in Lethbridge, Alberta and they homesteaded in the Carmangay area. Mother's full maiden name was Ellen Scott and she was born on September 7, 1888 to Elizabeth Ann Scott (née Snowdon) and William Turner Scott, both of Huddersfield, Yorkshire County, England. Dad's full name was Thomas Alfred Middleton and he was born on September 5, 1883 to Francis Harriet Middleton (née Pays) and Joseph Daniel Middleton, both of London, England. My mother's dad was Scottish and her mother was English. My dad's mother was French and his father was English.

Opposite page:

(top) My mother, Ellen Scott, (age 18)

(right) My dad, Thomas Alfred Middleton, (age 11 or 12)

(left) The family homestead, west of Carmangay by Little Bow River, fall 1911. Mother is holding Thelma and is expecting Francis.

Between 1911 and 1928, my parents had five children: Thelma Elizabeth, born June 2, 1911; Ellen Francis, born December 17, 1912; Walter Thomas, born August 26, 1915; Edna Grace, born July 18, 1917; and me, Mary Victoria, born June 3, 1928.

My mother was a delicate English lady, 5'2", with black hair and a lovely fair complexion. I think it must have been hard for her as a new bride in this windy country. Especially when in the first year of her marriage the floor of the house was dirt and they had to burn cow chips in the stove for fuel. Homesteading was very difficult in those early days.

Mother had a great love of gardening and especially of growing beautiful flowers. I can still see her sitting at our old black piano playing and singing hymns and other songs. She used to play "Acushla Mine" and "Brahm's Lullaby" and her favourite song, "In The Garden."

My dad, as I recall, always wore a big bushy moustache and his eyebrows were also bushy. He had a love for nature, animals and birds. In later years he received the homesteaders' scroll from the Alberta government. As a boy he sang in a church choir. My mother and dad were both very musical.

I found out years later that my mother's brother, Walter Scott, tried to homestead in Montana but he didn't like it and went back to England. When he died he left a small estate to my mother. I understand that the estate was in the hands of lawyers for 10 years, and they traced my mother's family tree and found out that she was distantly related to Anne Hathaway, who married William Shakespeare in 1582. Anne Hathaway was born in Shottery, a village about one mile from Stratford-on-Avon, England, where her famous cottage still remains.

Early Childhood

My recollections of my early years are vague and I can only recall certain incidents. I understand that the family moved from the homestead into Carmangay when I was eight months old. Carmangay was a small town of around 400 people and was mostly a farming community. The house we moved into was formerly Carmangay's first hospital.

My first memory is of being baptized at two or three years of age by Cannon T.B. Winter of the Anglican Church. I don't remember this part, but apparently, right after the Reverend

baptized me, I called him a "dumb nut!" Whoops. I was baptized during the Prohibition, and my mother took abstinence vows for me, which meant she vowed I would never drink alcohol. Another early memory I have is of seeing a thunderbolt during a summer storm. A big ball of fire sailed just over my head. I sat in my mother's lap all evening because this particular thunderstorm was so severe.

I can still see my mother's small frame bending over a big round pan punching down dough for homemade bread. I remember beautiful loaves of brown bread coming out of the coal and wood range. I used to help her with the washing, which was an all-day affair. Mother's knuckles were raw from scrubbing clothes on the washboard. Later on she got one of those machines you could work back and forth by hand. I also used to operate the churn to make butter for her. The dasher for the churn was an old broom handle with a crosspiece nailed on the bottom. The cream was put in an earthenware jar and you worked the dasher up and down in the cream until you got butter.

Our house was not very big. It had three bedrooms, a living room, a dining room and a very small kitchen. It was heated by a round pot-bellied stove in the living room and also by the kitchen stove. The sound that woke us up in the morning were Dad scraping the ashes down and putting wood and coal into the stove. We used the stove to heat water and to melt snow for washing our hair. Our water supply was a cistern under the dining room in a small basement you could get in by a trap door in the floor. We had no fridge or icebox in those days and Mother kept butter and milk cool in the basement. The pump and sink were in the dining room and all our wash and bath water was heated in a tub on the wood range. Saturday night, with the round wash tub in the middle of the kitchen, was our bathing time.

The Depression

The Depression years were very difficult. One in five families were on welfare. The price of wheat dropped to 25 cents a bushel. Our family didn't go on welfare but I know from many reports that we suffered. I was too young to realize the full impact of the times people were experiencing in those 10 years, but I remember some things like people coming to the door to ask for an egg or a piece of bread or anything they could get. I heard one man say, "I hate to beg and if there was any other way I wouldn't be begging."

There was great unemployment during the thirties so many men were riding the freight trains from town to town looking for work. Indians used to go from town to town by wagons, desperate for food or work. A group came to the house one day when mother had just taken a batch of bran muffins out of the oven. One woman said,

"I used to walk for miles along the river and carry her in my arms."

Mary's sister, Francis, 85

"Our brother Walter had a very hard time finding work. He "rode the rods," which meant that he rode freight trains trying to find some work."

Francis

Opposite page:
Dad and Mother, my sisters Francis (left), Thelma (right) and baby Walter

This page:
Me!

"One day, one of Dad's cows decided to wander about the town. She walked under a clothesline and ended up walking down Main Street with underwear over her face."

Francis

"I did very well in school. Mother and Dad decided to board me in town at $30 a month so I could get my grade 10. They wanted me to be a teacher, but times were very hard. We were just going into the real Depression years, so I had to quit after grade 11 and go out to work."

Francis

Opposite page:
Me at age 5 with my sister Edna

"Me take — good for my papoose." People were so desperate that one woman took my mother's sweater without asking. What could my mother do? It was probably the only sweater Mother owned at that time.

We lived on the edge of town so my dad was able to have a milk cow and a few chickens. Dad delivered eggs and milk, mended shoes, repaired clocks and drove horses for a water wagon — anything to keep the food on the table. He had two baskets he used to deliver milk around town. We had no car or horse and buggy. One time he was delivering to a place on the outskirts of town, after dark, and a pack of hungry coyotes came very close to him. I was very scared that night because I could hear those coyotes howling in the cold winter night. I was never very close to Dad and never felt like I knew him very well. I believe there were some problems and much of his spare time was spent away from the home.

The only doll I ever had as a child was from a relief society in Calgary. Dad gave me five cents a week for allowance. In the summertime after rainstorms, I would gather buckets of mushrooms and sell them. I didn't have many store-bought clothes, mostly hand-me-downs and what Mother could sew or make over. One Christmas, I overheard my parents say they really couldn't afford a Christmas tree but they better try and have one for Mary's sake. My sisters all had to quit school early and go out to work.

When I was really young, I saw a man accidentally electrocuted by overhead wires. I didn't know that he was being killed. I found out later, but as a child I didn't really know what it meant so it didn't have an impact at the time. I think children are sheltered from these things.

Still, in spite of hard times, there were many enjoyable experiences in those early years. I was very adventurous and liked nothing better than exploring the river hills, finding old caves, building campfires and roasting potatoes sneaked from home. I brought many pails of saskatoons home to my mother to make pies, jams and canned fruit. These river hills were also a source of much fun for tobogganing parties in the winter.

I Was a Tomboy

I was very active and tomboyish in nature. At the age of three I was pulled out from under the wheels of a freight train just seconds before they passed over where I was crawling. Frank Sabo was the name of the fellow who pulled me out by my feet. One time, I climbed inside the steel columns on the train bridge and felt the shaking as a train went over. Under the train bridge was the old swimming hole. I could swim ever since my brother and sisters threw me in at age six. One spring during the thaw, when the river was full and going very fast, I attempted to swim to an island in the middle. I never told my mother about that — I am sure she would have had a heart attack. Now it scares me to think of the foolish risk I took. I came close to losing my life that

"One time, my mom and I went to a shower for one of the girls I knew. We told Mary to stay home but she turned up anyway, and with a dirty neck and a dirty dress! I'll never forget that. She had a little stubborn streak in her. If you'd tell her to do something she wouldn't necessarily do it."

"She was always a girl that was busy, busy, busy. I looked after her. She'd run uptown and I'd run after her. Thelma loved Mary so much. Thelma looked out for all of us because Mother wasn't really able to. "

Mary's sister, Edna, 82

"That poor wee sister had so many bosses, she did not know which way to turn. She was never afraid of anything."

Francis

day. Another time I climbed onto the water tower so I could look for miles around the countryside. I was even active in my sleep. One night, I was sleep-walking and woke up sitting on the steps of the United Church, which was a block from my house. I was about six at the time.

While I am on the subject of climbing, I should say that my friends and I used to run along the tops of the train box cars while they were parked by the elevators. One time, I climbed onto the roof of a shed and tried to use an umbrella as a parachute. Another time I went out to Francis and her husband Roy's place and climbed the windmill, only this time I took Francis' daughter Audrey with me. She was only three or four years old at the time. When Roy saw us, the windmill paddles were about to turn and we could have both been knocked to the ground. Well, I think I may as well tell all. I got into the henhouse and threw all the setting eggs against the side of the building. No wonder Roy and Francis didn't have any baby chicks that year. Rest assured, I haven't heard the end of these things to this day!

Although my climbing sometimes got me into trouble, there were times when it saved me from trouble. For example, one time when a bull from one of the country farms stormed into the yard and chased me up a ladder onto the roof of our kitchen. I remained there a couple of hours before he went away.

A bit on the humorous side was the playhouse the neighbour kids and myself built in the backyard. It was made up of slabs of tin and cardboard. We experimented in that playhouse by smoking crushed tree leaves rolled in brown paper. Boy, the smoke poured out of the cracks and we soon quit that for fear of Dad or the neighbours catching us. And my dad told me if he ever caught me smoking, he would knock the cigarette out of my mouth and knock me down. No wonder I don't smoke to this day! Another playhouse I had was under a spreading maple tree by our garage. It was very pleasant there in the summertime. I had a hole in the ground for a cooler, and with a few dishes of sugar and butter from mother's cupboard, my tea parties were complete.

My dad used to raise canaries in a spare room. Some could sing so beautifully. When I was around 10 years of age, I decided that I would raise birds too, so I caught a baby sparrow and brought the poor little thing into the house. Well, in those days Dad had a milk cow and since we didn't have a cream separator, pans of milk were sitting all around in the dining room. In the morning the cream was taken off to make butter and the skim milk was made into cottage cheese. To get back to my sparrow, it got loose from the spare room and drowned in a pan of milk, ending my bird raising, at least for a few years.

Opposite page:
(top) *Age 7 with my dog Curly*

(bottom) *My brother Walter, (early 20's)*

This page:
Age 7, on the porch of our house

My Dog Curly

At an early age I owned a big black curly-haired dog named Curly. I used to ride Curly all over town. Then one day he was chasing a Greyhound bus and a rock flew up and embedded between his eyes. He was killed instantly. I screamed all the way home. It took me a while to get over that.

My Sisters and Brother

I don't remember too much of living with my sisters and brother, as they went out to work and got married while I was still quite young. I do recall a few incidents when everyone was at home. One of my sisters (I think it was Francis) put her elbows on the table and Dad tapped them with the back handle of a knife. Another time, everyone was sitting at the old round table doing homework, reading and whatever, and a roaring argument broke out. I can still see how fast Dad moved to make everyone sit off in the corners of the room. I can't even remember what that fight was about. Oh well, all families have their ups and downs.

There was quite an age difference between my three older sisters and me. I remember causing them a great deal of embarrassment when the boyfriends came to call. I would crawl on their laps and ask for gum. I got a severe reprimand after they left. "You don't ask for gum — that's not nice." So of course the next time the boyfriends arrived, I didn't ask for gum, I only walked around them exclaiming, "I *smell* gum."

Later on, sometimes I was the one who got embarrassed. In those days there wasn't any indoor plumbing, so the thing to do was to have a wee potty under the bed. One Sunday afternoon my brother Walter decided it was time to empty the thing, so with pot extended in front of him he marched into the dining room. Suddenly he realized my boyfriend was there and all Walter could do was say, "Whoops," turn on his heel and quickly make his exit. I can laugh about this now but then I was mortified.

"Our sister was given the name Edna Daisy Middleton, which was later changed to Edna Grace Middleton, after she discovered that the family milk cow shared her middle name."

Francis

Walter was always very much interested in radio. He made an amateur radio transmitting and receiving set in his bedroom. He spent hours and hours studying and building his ham radio set. He spoke to other amateur hams from all over the country. An exciting event in our home was getting our first radio. That evening, we all gathered around it and we heard our first program. Among some of my favourite shows were "Fibber McGee and Molly," "Superman" and "Major Bowles' Talent Show."

School Days

Carmangay had a typical little red brick schoolhouse that was two stories with a large bell on top. It had a separated basement, one side for boys and one side for girls. There were four classrooms with three grades in each. We also had a small chemistry lab and a room under the bell tower for typing and sewing courses. The toilets were outdoor wooden structures, and we didn't have toilet tissue in those days, so we used old Eaton's catalogues or newspapers.

School had its ups and downs. Seems I was always getting put in front of or behind this certain boy, Harvey Robertson. I swear he ate all my pencils and drank my glue, and kept bugging me by whipping my legs with his ruler. What a pest he was. Now, I heard in later years, he is over 200 pounds. No wonder! Another little kid in grade one poured a bottle of glue over his own head. Very good hair dressing, he thought. I will always remember this particularly fat boy in grade six yelling at the top of his voice, "Please may I go to the washroom? My mother fed me on salts (laxatives) last night!"

Speaking of mothers, mine, being a very dutiful person, took very good care to see what I wore to school. Sometimes, I had to wear navy blue fleece-lined bloomers and long stockings with over-the-shoulder garters. How I hated wearing those!

I got the strap in grade two for cheating that I wasn't guilty of. My arms were black and blue up to my elbows. My parents were very angry at the teacher and for many years I didn't hold very kind thoughts towards her. To this day I feel that strapping was unjustified. I failed grade two. I don't know why. That's the year I had a cranky teacher.

Since we are on the subject of strappings, I recall the one and only strapping my dad gave me. I was around seven and I had poured a can of cold rain water down this poor, demented neighbour lady's neck. You could hear her yell all over town. My bottom and legs were red when Dad got through with me. My poor timid mother stood in the door looking on.

Outstanding events in my early school days were the Christmas concerts and the hours of practice for them. We did the traditional Nativity scene, plays, skits, songs and piano playing. At the end of the concert, Santa came to give out candy bags.

In grade six I thought I would help Mother Nature along by wearing my mother's falsies to school. Of course the drastic change was noted by all, and before long I was the brunt of much teasing. The next day I came to school my old flat-chested self.

Mother Was Never Very Strong

When I was 12 my mother had a nervous breakdown. I remember very clearly being called home from the community hall where we were practicing for a Christmas concert. In the living room there was a policeman, a judge, Dad, and Mother. They were signing papers. I was very confused. Anyway, Mother was taken away to a hospital in Ponoka and was gone for three months. They gave her shock treatments. Dad and I went by train once to visit her. The only thing I remember about that trip was the mentally ill people locked in a room and screaming. I looked in a small window and they had no clothes on. Mother wasn't in there. She just sat in a chair quiet and withdrawn. It was a very confusing time for me. A time when I didn't really understand. I think mother had rather a hard life. She was never very strong.

Opposite page:
(top left) Mother, 1946

(top right) Dad, 1947

(bottom) Dad, me (age 16) and Mother, taken at Edna and Wilf's. Edna gave me the dress.

My Dad was not a good cook. Many a day, I would come home from school and all we would have to eat was pickled pig's feet or tripe, which is boiled cow's stomach. I didn't like any of these things. My father never believed too much in doctors. Being plagued by bronchitis I was always sure to get one of his famous doses of raw egg, lemon, and honey, mostly always in the middle of the night. He must have often been too tired to mix it very good and that slimy raw egg still makes me shudder when I think of it. Thankfully, sometimes Francis and Roy would take me out to their farm where the cooking was better.

Teen Years

There was a Chinese restaurant in Carmangay called the Club Café, which was a major meeting place. There was also a theatre that cost 25 cents for a movie. This was where I saw the first moving pictures. That was a real social thing we did. We had Sunday school picnics with sack races and things like that. You know in a small town, this is what you did for entertainment. We also had an annual fair called the Carmangay Stampede. There was a Ferris wheel and other small rides. I used to go to the fair grounds the day after the Stampede to look for money where the grandstands were.

On a more serious note, World War II was on when I was a teenager. A lot of things were rationed. For example, we had coupons in order to buy a little bit of sugar. I remember rolling up the toothpaste holders, which were made out of lead in those days. Maybe they were melted down for bullets or something. I don't know for sure. We also saved all rubber products. It was sent away somewhere.

On weekends I used to go by train 10 miles to Champion to stay with my sister Edna and her husband Wilfred. I remember eating a whole pile of corn at their place! One time, when I went to sit down on the train, the clasp on my cardboard suitcase gave 'way and my pajamas and underwear went rolling down the aisle, along with my jar of Noxema. The train was full of soldiers. Several of them quickly retrieved the articles for me and I went on my way. I was 12 or 13, just old enough to be terribly mortified!

In 1945, when they announced that the war was over, all of us teenagers made an effigy of Hitler and burned it on a pile of railroad ties. It was a huge bonfire. My brother was a signal corps operator on the front lines in Holland. He had a nervous breakdown and was sent to England to convalesce. While there, he made bracelets from copper pennies. He sent me one. He also wrote poetry and sent it home to the local newspaper. Now, some of these poems are read at local Remembrance Day services.

"I was never very close to dad and never felt like I knew him very well. Mother was never very strong."

Mary

"She would stay and I'd give her some of my old clothes. I gave her my wedding dress. Wilf nearly had a fit, but I wanted her to have it."

Edna

"Walter saw his chum Harold Smith, son of a United Church minister in Carmangay, killed a few feet in front of him. When he returned, he was so thin, he was all eyes, and the tension he had been through was so bad, he was holding his neck with his hands."

Francis

"Rest! Rest! You have stood the test, but never a war did you suggest. Your time ends now, the Motherland calls, from peace to war, our country falls."

Excerpt of a poem by Mary's brother Walter, now 84

Opposite page:
School friends, 1944

This page:
Omer, my long-necked boyfriend

Going Out With Boys

When I was 15 I went to stay with my oldest sister Thelma and her husband Emil at Iron Springs. They had two girls, Lorraine and Edna Faye. We used to go swimming in the irrigation ditch. One day a boy came along on horseback. Pretty soon he became a frequent visitor. He had a very long neck and we used to say maybe his mother ran him through the wringer on the washing machine. Well, anyway, he got quite a crush on me and had big plans for the future. He often said, "Poor pony, my horse will surely be swaybacked with two people riding on him all the time." His name was Omer Sonnenen. He had a long name like his long neck. So much for my encounter with one of my first boyfriends. There was also another boy interested from the same area. It sounds like I am making this up, but honest to God I'm not, his name was Stewart Dickout. Oh well, what's in a name?

When I was 15 or 16 years of age I was still going to school, working in the telephone office, playing basketball, and going out with boys. Mother was not well mentally and she was terrified something terrible would happen to me. She didn't want me to go out. It was upsetting for me as a teenager trying to grow up under these kinds of conditions. I must have got around this because I remember doing lots of things. I failed grade nine. My mother was in and out of the hospital. I suppose my attention span wasn't very good. But I went on to pass with honours the next year.

Chicken Changers Ride the Range

One Sunday evening six of us teenagers went joy-riding. I don't even recall who the kids were or whose idea it was but we first raided a local garden for a few carrots, then went on into the countryside. We thought it would be fun if we went to one farmer's place and took six chickens and moved them to the chicken coop at the next farm. Then we'd take six of this farmer's chickens and so on. Now, in theory this sounded really good so we managed to do this at two places but at the third place the lights went on and the dog barked so we quickly ran for the car and on the way one of the boys grabbed a turkey, which was roosting in a tree.

We drove very fast back to Carmangay and hid in the back alley behind the hotel. The police were called and we could see them going up and down Main Street. We stayed in the alley real late, wondering what we were going to do with that turkey. Suddenly, we remembered that there was still a rooster in the trunk. So what we did is drive to the teacherage (a house where the local teachers lived) and put the turkey and the rooster in the back porch. It was so late when I got home, I had to crawl in my bedroom window so my parents wouldn't hear me.

Well, the next day after school I had to work in the telephone office. When the red button showed on the board, I plugged into it and said, "number, please." Then I connected this woman with the party she wanted. Now, there was a switch on the board that I could turn on and hear their conversation. Well, you will never guess what I heard! One woman said, "You know, when I went to feed my chickens this morning, there were six white leghorns mixed in with my Plymouth Rock chickens!" And the other woman said that, yes, one of their turkeys was missing also and what a mystery it was.

Well, this story has a unique ending. The next weekend my boyfriend Bob and I were invited to the teachers' house for Thanksgiving dinner. Throughout the meal, they were remarking about the kindness of someone leaving them a rooster and a turkey. Many years later, Carmangay school had a 30-year reunion and two of the teachers were there. I confessed to them what we did and all they could say was, "My god, it was you kids that did that!"

So much for one of my teenage escapades. I want you to know we didn't intend to steal that night, only mix up the farmers' chickens but it did end up we got stuck with one turkey and one rooster.

The Hole Story

There was no indoor plumbing in the town, so all the homes had outhouses out back, complete with an Eaton's catalogue. Around Christmas, there might be wrappers off oranges for a special treat! One Halloween, a bunch of us went around town pushing over outhouses, which was a common prank. There were cases of people getting pushed over while in the outhouse. We tipped over two or three, and on the fourth, well, this gentleman knew we'd be around, so he moved his outhouse a few feet and left the old hole open. We girls didn't try to push on that outhouse, so it was all the boys who fell in the hole! Ha! As luck would have it, it was very cold, and the contents of the hole were frozen.

The Girls' Club

I belonged to a girls' sewing club for a few years, which was sponsored by the Olds' Agricultural School. Me and Norma Munks and two younger girls won a scholarship to go for two weeks to the Agriculture School where there were girls from all over Alberta. We displayed our sewing and put on programs. The four of us got up and performed, "I'm a Little Teapot." I'll never forget that! While we were there, we took short courses in beekeeping, cooking, sewing and so on. I was 18 at the time. After

"Oh dear! I do remember roasting a turkey but I didn't know where it came from."

Helen (Bewes) Newton, 84, a former high school teacher, immediately after hearing that she had once unknowingly cooked a stolen turkey for Thanksgiving

"I remember how keen she was on doing a good job of her work."

Helen (Bewes) Newton former leader of the girls' club

this, we were selected to go into a contest where we were up against other teams to compete for a free trip to the World's Fair, which was being held in Toronto that year. We missed going by only one point! You know what we fell down on? The verbal part! We did well on the sewing and the writing part. Oh well, you can't always be the best.

While I was in the girls' club, one of the items I sewed was a two-piece bathing suit, which was a big no-no in those days. It was a blue-flowered suit. Why, the first time I wore it, I was diving off a diving board and the bottom half flew off as soon as I hit the water. Good thing it got caught on my big toe for a second, and I was able to get hold of it before it left for parts unknown. I quickly scrambled to get it back on. Thankfully, no one was the wiser. Doing my own sewing, I guess I didn't have it exactly right.

Meeting and Getting Engaged to Bob Long

My first big crush was on a fellow named Jim Carlson from Champion. He was Mormon, and I think when the parents thought the relationship was too steady they discouraged it. It was about that time Bob Long come along. He was hauling grain to the elevators in Carmangay and courting at the same time. One time, we were out at a restaurant eating raisin pie and I lifted up the top crust and pretended that I saw cockroaches. I started whacking the table and saying, "cockroaches! cockroaches!" The proprietor of the restaurant overheard me and he came over and said, "I'll have you know, young lady, there are no cockroaches in *this* restaurant!" I was so embarrassed. Years later, I found out that Bob hated raisin pie and just ordered it because he thought it was proper for the boy to order the same thing as the girl.

Bob taught me to drive on a two-ton truck. Early on, I turned my wheel too sharp on a corner and ended up going in the ditch and out into a farmer's field. Luckily, there was no fence. When I was going out with Bob he wrote this in my autograph book: I had a date with Mary at three, her organs internal made noises infernal and everyone thought it was me!

In high school, I enjoyed playing basketball and I liked art, music and language. But I left school after I finished half of grade 11. I think I just lost interest. Mother wasn't around. I guess I just didn't have the encouragement to stay on. Bob and I set our wedding date for February 14, 1947. I was only 18 and Bob was not quite 21. We

Opposite page:

(top) Courting days for me and Bob, 1946. Bob taught me to drive on a two-ton truck

(bottom) Bob and I shortly before eating Thanksgiving dinner at the teacherage, 1946

This page:

Age 18, achievement day for the Girls' Club, sponsored by the Olds Agricultural School, 1946

were much too young. Not even dry behind the ears. I thought a lot of Bob at the time but I can see that maybe getting married so young was to escape a difficult situation at home.

Helen Bewes and Marie Matlock, two of my school teachers, held a wedding shower for me. These teachers really stand out for me. So does the principal, Leonard McKenzie. I think that in those days, students and teachers were much closer. They knew I was having a hard time with my mother being away so much. They seemed to pay some extra attention to me.

The shower was an absolute scream. When I came in, they made me sit on a stool in the middle of the room. The stool was covered with a blanket. No one said a word, so then I started asking questions like, "Why aren't you saying anything?" "What's under the blanket?" Every time I opened my mouth to say anything, the whole room went into gales of laugher. After several minutes, they told me that these were the things I would say on my wedding night!

"It's a lot of years ago, but I remember that Mary was a very special girl and a very sweet person. It was easy to do nice things for her. I always liked Mary. I knew that her home life was hard, that she had things to contend with there. But she had a way of figuring things out. Some people would have been down and blue, but Mary just wasn't like that."

Marie (Matlock) Granlin, 84, a former teacher of Mary's

2

On the Move: Early Married Life
1947 to 1957

B ob and I were married in Lethbridge at a Pentecostal church. There were 30 people at our wedding reception, which was held at the Marquis Hotel in Lethbridge. Mother could not come, as she just couldn't face losing her Mary. That's what she said: "I have lost you." In the evening we held a wedding dance at the community hall. The hall was packed.

On the day of our wedding, there was what they call a sudden chinook, which melted a lot of snow. The Model T Ford we were riding in had holes in the floor and the bottom of my wedding dress got soaking wet. I had sandals on my feet, so they were wet too. Water was gushing across the roads and the roads weren't like they are now, so some roads washed through.

Our honeymoon was spent in Calgary. After a week, the weather turned to 20° below (Fahrenheit) and we tried to drive home. Now, we decided to go across country but at least some of the roads had been under water and were frozen over. We came to this patch of ice, tried driving over it, but broke through. It was about 9:00 at night, very dark, and we must have walked half a mile or so, till we came to a farmhouse.

The people were surprised when we showed up on their doorstep. They took us in and got a pail of snow to put my frozen feet in. They say now that this is the wrong procedure, but we didn't know at the time. The next day the farmer got his tractor going and pulled our Model T Ford out of the ice.

Camping in Bear Country

In the summer of 1947, before Bob and I had any kids, we went on a fishing trip with the Schramm couple. I can't remember their first names now. We drove down to Waterton Lake, then on to the US border. We went to a very remote area called the

Opposite page:
The Claresholm farm

This page:
Our first wedding anniversary, February 14, 1948

"I bet you didn't know that your mother was so long-winded. I never dreamt I could remember so much. Things keep popping up. On with the tail. Ha! I mean tale. "

Mary, in her notes to Ellen about writing this book, 1998

Slide Lake area. It was called Slide Lake because a mountain slide cut a lake in two. There were very rugged roads, rutted and rocky. We got out our fishing gear and spent a happy, carefree time fishing.

Well, we never noticed black clouds rolling in and on the first clap of thunder, we leaped up and, oh my gosh, did we scramble to get out of there. It was about half a mile up the road and buckets of rain came down. The roads turned to mud and slop and in grinding through this, the low gear went out of the old truck. We managed to get off the road a few feet and the boys pitched the tent beside the road. It was dark and very scary. The boys got the camp stove in and we made supper.

After supper there was nothing to do but crawl into our sleeping bags. It was very damp and steamy in the tent. Bob's friend started telling stories about when he and his dad had been bear hunting. Well, just as he was finishing his story we realized we had a bear by our tent! Of course we were dumb, naive young people and we had food in our tent. What to do? So one of the men lifted up the tent flap and hollered "Woof!" and shone his flashlight in the bear's face. Boy, did that bear take off to parts unknown! After that, I began to shake and none of us could sleep all night.

In the morning two sheep herders came along. They told how lucky we were, as this was grizzly bear country we just camped in! This is where the cranky bears from the national parks were let loose. They also told us they had killed a grizzly bear in

this area the day before and its paws were as big as a woman's purse. Anyway, we loaded up our truck and the two sheep herders who had a jeep pulled us out of there backwards. Boy, was I ever glad to get home and I don't think you ever got me to sleep in the mountains again in a tent. Some fishing experience!

By the way, we were pulled to a garage, and the repairs cost about $200, which was a lot of money in those days.

The Claresholm Farm

When we were first married, we lived on a farm around Claresholm where we had a two-room house in Bob's parents' yard. I didn't have a clue how to cook so Mom Long took me under her wing and proceeded to teach me how to cook, raise chickens and tend a garden. She was a very warm and wonderful woman. She also had a very good sense of humour. I loved and respected her very much.

High River

After the fall work was done in the same year we were married, Bob could not get along with his dad, so we left. Bob got a job as second man (an apprentice elevator operator) for the United Grain Growers Company in High River. We moved into a small two-room cabin and I had to scrub clothes on a washboard after heating the wash water on the stove. During the winter of '47-'48, I worked every day in Laycrafts Drug Store. They had a soda fountain bar with a counter and about a half-dozen stools. I made banana splits, milkshakes and sodas.

Whiskey Gap

In the spring of '48, Bob got his first elevator posting in a small place called Whiskey Gap. It was just a few miles from the US border crossing of Del Bonita. For entertainment that winter we played bridge. Sometimes we would go down to the States. We went for a weekend down to a town called Cutbank with Bob's brother Ken and his wife, Mary. In the Gap, we lived by ourselves on a side hill. Half a mile away were the elevators, one store, a post office, and about six houses. It was a fairly lonely place for a young person. In the summertime we drove to Waterton Park. That was nice. I can't remember how long we lived in Whiskey Gap. Maybe it was a year or two.

Back to the Claresholm Farm

I guess it was around that time that Bob's folks came down and asked us to go back to farming. We moved into the big farmhouse, as the folks bought a house in Claresholm. While we were there, Ken and Mary moved into the little house. There we were, two Mary Longs. So the family called me "Joe," and they called Mary "Frankie." Years later my kids called her Aunt Frankie and her kids called me Auntie Joe. Mary and I always hit it off and have remained friends all of our lives.

"I remember visiting at their home on the premises of Bob's parents. Of course it was neat as a pin. Marie (Matlock) and I went out to their place in Whiskey Gap for supper one night. It was a pleasant evening. Bob was quite a good visitor, you know."

Helen (Bewes) Newton

Opposite page:
Here I am (far right) with my 3 sisters and one of my nieces, 1948

This page:
Life on the farm, 1947

"If it hadn't been for Mary (Joe) at that time, I don't know what I would have done. She was there to support me. After we got through talking, things never seemed so bad."

Frankie (Mary), Mary's sister in-law, 72

Opposite page:

Melvin Douglas Long, June 21, 1950 to July 22, 1950

Melvin's grave, Claresholm, Alberta

This page:

I made a snowman after a major snowstorm in June!

I remember one outstanding snowstorm on June 5, 1951. There was power lines down all over Alberta. I went out and made a snowman, put a placard on its chest and took a picture. I have the picture as proof. I also remember Ken, Pa Long, Bob and some neighbour men digging up a coyote den and bringing out five or six snarling pups.

I enjoyed farm life. When I was pregnant with my first baby, I got 400 baby chicks and also had a big garden. I remember one time, I wanted to go out at noon and run the tractor. It was a small tractor. We called it the puddle jumper. It had two big wheels on back and two small wheels in the front. Anyway, this one time, I got on the tractor and started cultivating the corn. I was so happy I never looked behind and suddenly I saw something in front of me. "What's that ahead of me?" I wondered. It was the cultivator! It had become unhitched and I never knew it. Some farmer I turned out to be. I got lots of ribbing over that.

Melvin Douglas

When I was 22 years of age, our first child, Melvin Douglas Long, was born on June 21, 1950. Baby Melvin was a beautiful, healthy baby so it broke our hearts when he died one month and one day later. He started having spells, turning blue and screaming till he almost passed out. I took him to the doctor and he told me that I was a nervous young mother. A few days later, Melvin died. I was tormented for a long time and didn't know until the next summer what the true cause of death was. I thought I had done something stupid to cause his death. Even as I write this, the sadness floods back and the tears flow. What a grievous thing it is to lose one's child.

For physical reasons, I had to quit nursing and I started using the well water for Melvin's formula. Turns out, the well water was contaminated with nitrates, which apparently doesn't bother nursing babies but is harmful to bottle-fed babies. These

---

Recipe for Walnut Squares
We really used to enjoy this recipe of Mary's! Helen (Bewes) Newton, former school teacher.

Part One

2 cups flour (sifted)
¾ cup butter
¼ cup brown sugar (packed)

Cream the butter and sugar, add the flour, and pack the mixture into a nine-inch-square pan. Bake at 300° F for 15-20 minutes.

Part Two

1½ cups brown sugar
2 tbsp flour
1 tsp. Baking power
pinch salt
1 cup chopped walnuts
½ cup shredded coconut
1 tsp vanilla
2 eggs

Sift the brown sugar; mix it with flour, baking powder and salt. Add the chopped walnuts, coconut, vanilla, and beaten eggs and mix together. Pour mixture over part one and bake at 350° F for about 40 minutes.

Mrs. Mary Long
from The Rinard Merry Makers' Cookbook, published by a women's club that Mary belonged to in Whiskey Gap
Provided by Helen (Bewes) Newton

nitrates get into the well water from the fields of corn that were grown on the farm. The summer rains leach them into the water table. Only some wells get this condition and people should get their wells checked if there are large fields of corn around and they can't nurse their babies.

My beautiful baby, Melvin Douglas, is buried in Claresholm. His funeral was held at the folks' home in Claresholm. The song "Beyond the Sunset" was played at his funeral.

Beyond the Sunset

Song played at
Melvin Douglas Long's Funeral

Beyond the sunset, O blissful morning,

When with our Saviour heav'n is begun.

Earth's toiling ended, O glorious dawning;

Beyond the sunset when day is done.

Beyond the sunset no clouds will gather,

No storms will threaten, no fears annoy;

O day of gladness, O day unending,

Beyond the sunset, eternal joy!

Beyond the sunset a hand will guide me

To God the Father, whom I adore;

His glorious presence, His words of welcome,

Will be my portion on that fair shore.

Beyond the sunset, O glad reunion,

With our dear loved ones who've gone before;

In that fair homeland we'll know no parting,

Beyond the sunset for evermore!

"When I was about eight or nine, I stumbled across a picture of Melvin while I was playing in the basement. I was immediately overcome with a flood of emotion. I don't even know if I'd ever been told about the existence of this baby, but I could see from the pictures that he was my brother. Mom rarely spoke of this terrible tragedy. I think of Melvin often."

Ellen, Mary's daughter

"I can only imagine the loss they must have felt. Today, Melvin would be approaching 50 years old. I would have liked the opportunity to have known him. However, I am sure that day is coming."

David, Mary's son

Catherine Anne

The next year Catherine Anne Long was born on September 14, 1951. I was 23 years old. Cathy was a breach birth so she spent 24 hours in an oxygen incubator. She was a beautiful eight-pound, four-ounce baby girl. She had medium brown hair with a little tuft on top. I used to tie a ribbon on the top of her head. I enjoyed dressing her up in frilly dresses. Cathy was a very good child and I remember her having an incredible memory. We had a hired girl at the time, as I wasn't very strong. She was a Dutch girl named Minka.

Calgary

After Cathy was born we stayed at the farm over the winter, and in the spring of 1953, due to Pa and Bob not getting along, we left the farm and moved to Calgary. We were there a few months while we waited for Bob to get a posting with a grain company. We were in an upstairs apartment. I remember one time when Cathy was about eight months old and she was sleeping on the chesterfield. I went outside a minute and accidentally locked the door. Well, I panicked! I ran to a corner garage and they got a ladder and went in one of the apartment windows. Cathy slept through the whole thing!

We lived in Southwest Calgary, and one Sunday I went to Scarborough United Church. I was lonely and no one spoke to me. I didn't go back.

Opposite page:
(top) Cathy (age 6) grade 1

(bottom) Linda, about 12 months old, 1955

This page:
(top left) I'm 24, Cathy is 14 months, 1952

(top right) Bob and I with Catherine Anne at 2 months old, 1951

(right) Pa and Granny Long with Cathy (right) and other grandchildren, 1952

Judson

After we left Calgary, Bob got an elevator posting with the Alberta Pacific Grain Company at a siding called Judson. A siding is a small place on the outside of a larger centre, which has grain elevators and only a few houses. Judson was 25 miles southeast of Lethbridge. At first, we couldn't get in the big house because the elevator operator Bob was replacing had not moved yet. So we were in a two-room shack for awhile. One time, a weasel got in the shack and scared the living daylights out of me. Bob chased it out with a broom!

One Saturday night, Bob was bathing in a washtub in the middle of the kitchen, and in walked a Hutterite man. You see, our elevator was central to three Hutterite colonies and a lot of Bob's customers were Hutterites. After we moved into the big house, it was not unusual for me to have a living room of Hutterites. Now, television was invented and we got our first television. Boy, then did they come! They brought us fresh bread, fish and wine. To tell the truth, I got a little tired of this scene.

While at Judson, I raised a nice garden. We had a milk cow — a Jersey one at that. Once, I decided I would try to milk her. I guess I must have pinched her because she kicked and everything went sprawling — milk, stool, bucket and me. I never went back to try milking again. I don't think I would've made a good farm wife! One summer I decided to raise geese. They slept under the back porch. Every time someone come, these geese ran up the sidewalk screeching their heads off. How awful. Nobody could hear a word anyone said. In October, their heads came off and I proceeded to pluck them in the basement. I didn't have a clue what I was doing so I had goose down up my nose, on the ceiling, on the walls, and in every crack and crevice. What a nightmare. That was indeed my first and very last experience in raising geese.

"We had a tire swing in Judson that was quite a lot of fun. I took tap-dancing and ballet lessons."

Cathy, Mary's daughter

Linda Lorraine

During this time I became pregnant with Linda. A month before she was born, Bob got in a car accident. His ankle twisted under the brake pedal of the car. I think he broke it badly or crushed some bones. Linda Lorraine Long, weighing in at 10 pounds, was born in a Catholic hospital in Lethbridge on April 30, 1954. Another beautiful baby girl. Linda was born with thick black hair and was such a fat, cute baby. At a year old, I had to give her a hair cut because her hair was so long. In later years, she turned out to be a medium blond. I was 25 years of age when Linda was born.

Linda was a much more active child than Cathy. When she was around a year old, she fell downstairs and broke her collarbone. Then later she was climbing a cupboard and split her chin open so badly that she had to get stitches. Another time, when she would have been two or three years old, I went in the living room and here she was crawling along the top of the black piano and pictures were going every which way! Our house was heated by diesel oil and I believe it was bad for Linda and me, as our bronchitis was very bad there.

One evening, we were playing crib with our neighbour, Pete Weber. When he went to the washroom, Bob and I stacked

his hand to make a score of 29. This is the highest possible score you can get in crib and it's quite rare to get it. Well, Pete was so excited, he insisted that we phone the local radio station so they could announce it. Because he was so happy, we didn't have the heart to tell him the truth. We never did tell him, and I guess he went to his grave at the age of 90 thinking he once had a 29 hand in crib.

"My first life's memory is of Old Pete's house and of Pete himself, down the railway track from our house at Judson siding. I remember the musty smell of Pete's shack. I liked him."

Linda, Mary's daughter

One Easter I dressed Cathy and Linda in blue sheer material dresses and bought them Easter bonnets. The neighbour kids used to come over to play in our swimming pool in the summer.

During our time in Judson, Bob and I took in a boy called Ronnie Veres. He was about nine or ten years of age. His mother was put in a mental hospital and the sister couldn't cope with the large family, so we took Ronnie in.

Ida Marie

Again I became pregnant, this time with Ida. About this time we hired an older man named Charlie. When I was 29 years old, Ida Marie Long was born in Lethbridge on September 10, 1957, weighing in at nine pounds, four ounces. Once again, a baby with loads of black hair and very cute and chubby. When we came home from the hospital, I became very ill with Asian flu. I couldn't change Ida or feed her. I could barely get from the bed to a chair. Charlie took over for a few days till I got on my feet. Ida was born with a red birthmark on half of one foot but after a few months it went away.

Cathy was six years old, Linda was three, and Ida was a few months, when the course of our lives changed very drastically. Bob was in some kind of trouble with the police in Lethbridge. I never knew too much detail and I won't go into it, but anyway, he lost his bond with the grain company and lost his job. After taking a trip to Hinton near the mountains, we left Southern Alberta and Bob got a job as a backhoe operator in Hinton. This is the end of this chapter in our lives. Seven places in a few short years. As you can see, Bob was a mover, and it's not all told yet.

Opposite page:
Ida Marie at 8 or 9 months, 1958

This page:
(above left) "Old Pete" with Cathy (4) and Linda (2)

(above) Cathy, Ronnie Veres and Linda

2
Photo Album

Our truck lost its low gear when we were on holidays.

Our house in Judson

*We often skated on the dugout by the Claresholm farm.
Left to right: Bob's sister Mildred, Bob's brother Ken and sister-in-law
Mary (Frankie), me, and Bob's sister Eileen, winter 1948.*

*Cathy, age
2 or 3 years,
Judson*

*Linda Lorraine,
about 12 months,
Judson, 1955*

Cathy's first birthday party, Judson, 1952

Linda, Judson, 1955

Our neighbour Pete Weber riding a bike in Judson, mid-1950s

Ronnie pulling Linda in a wagon while Cathy oversees.

Cathy, Linda and two neighbour kids

Cathy with "McDuff"

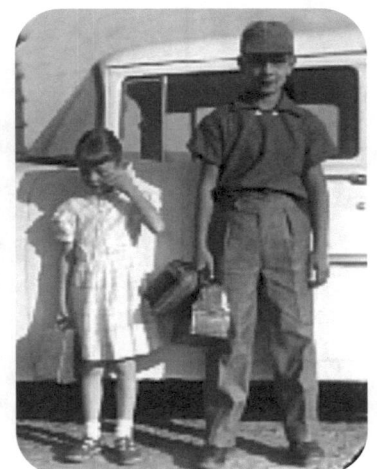

Cathy and Ronnie Veres
on their first day of school

Cathy and Ronnie

Cathy and Linda in outfits I made for them

3

The Joy and the Pain: Hinton — 1957 to 1961

Hinton was quite a change from southern Alberta. We moved to an apartment in a six-plex, in between two other apartments. This turned out to be very interesting: on one side lived a Dutch family and on the other side, a French couple. Well, every once in a while they had these rousing good fights. The walls were thin but that didn't matter because I couldn't understand a word they said anyway.

I met some of my other neighbours. The nicest ones were the Gledhills, an English couple, and their two children. They were fresh out of England and we had many a good laugh at some of their expressions. An example was the lady was always "knocking her husband up" in the morning or "packing his jock" for work.

One day, while living in the apartment, I accidentally grabbed a tube of hair dressing (Brill Creme) and brushed my teeth with it. I was almost ill.

Time to move again, only this time, within the same town, to a house a few blocks away. While in that house Bob, who was working on a backhoe, hurt his back and had to quit. Things were very uncertain. Money for rent and food was needed. Bob decided to apprentice under Nels Rutund, an older barber. Well, some of Bob's haircuts left something to be desired so money was scarce.

"I remember going on mountain picnics and picking a lot of wildflowers in the bushes at Hinton."
I saved up my allowance and bought a little fishing rod so I could fish in a stream by our house."

Cathy

Opposite page:
Bob and I (ages 31 and 33) Ronnie (age 13 or 14) and the girls (8, 5, and about 2) Hinton, 1959

This page:
Bob, Ronnie, the girls (9, 6, 3) and I, Hinton, October, 1960

Spiritual Awakening

My faith in God was weaker in those days. I didn't know God, or couldn't feel him — it seemed I was just talking to empty air. I knew all I had been taught by my mother but didn't ever have a personal experience myself. Times were so unsure for us so one Saturday I went to a newly built United Church. The first thing held in this new church was a wedding. I will always remember the profound experience I had during that wedding service. God touched my soul — I was like a sheep skipping over the fields that day and I felt a new sense of hope and strength to face the future. I went home, got the three children, and went to the mountains for a picnic. The next week I took in three boarders and started to cook up a storm. It helped the budget till Bob got better at cutting hair.

I loved Hinton for the natural beauty of the area. We would go swimming in Miette Hot Springs, or drive to Jasper and explore the beauty of the mountains. Unfortunately, Hinton was the home of a large pulp mill. When the wind was right, or the weather turned cold, the fumes were something terrible.

During this time I never forgot the beautiful experience I had that day in church, so I bought a beautiful set of Bible story books. I read them all, and I read them to my children. I also remember studying the letters of St. Paul. I went to church and met some real nice people named Jack and Jean Harstone.

> "She had the strongest influence on me of anyone else in my life. She had amazingly strong faith, and my wife Linda and I have faith today because of her example.
>
> Ronnie Veres, 52, lived with Mary and Bob for about three years

> "I remember the concrete being poured for the sidewalk in front of our new home. I was told not to walk on it. Of course, I went right over and did it, leaving a nice footprint! "
>
> Linda

> "I remember the excitement of buying the new house. The man next door had a stucco business and he would pay us kids a nickel for those blue-coloured Milk of Magnesia and Vicks bottles, which he crushed to use as prized pieces in his stucco mixtures. "
>
> Cathy

> "I remember being able to breathe in Hinton and taking delight in that. I couldn't breathe in Judson. Now I know that I was asthmatic and reacting to the dust in Southern Alberta."
>
> Linda

LESSONS

My mother taught me the love of quiet things,
The whisper of the hummingbird's wings,
The quietude of twinkling stars in the sky,
The silence of snowflakes drifting by.

My mother taught me the love of pretty things,
Beautiful art in butterfly wings,
God-given rainbows, the flowers and the trees,
  And grasses gently bent by the breeze.

My mother taught me the love of singing things,
Sweet musical voices ..... violin strings,
Melodies sung by birds at breaking dawn,
The soft sigh of the wind all night long.

My mother taught me the love of human beings,
The joy that a little baby brings,
The unbroken love of life tried o'er and o'er,
The thrill of friendhsip's knock at the door.

Dorothy Jane Buchan

A Home of Our Own

Bob was getting to be a very good barber so things were going a lot better. The folks came up from Claresholm. They were always there to help us get ahead. They offered to back us in buying a home of our own. We bought a house on the hill. Before, we lived in the valley part of Hinton. Our new house was a ranch-style home with pretty stonework half up the front. I used to take the kids to the mountains to gather black shale rock to go around the flower beds. Then I would dig up wild tiger lilies for around the house. I remember that the Christmas trees we had were huge and reached the ceiling. I haven't had one like those since. I was so thrilled to have our own house. I don't even have a picture of it. I didn't mention, when we first moved to Hinton, we had to send Ronnie Veres back to his family. When we moved into our own place, we sent for him again.

Around this time, I become pregnant with Ellen. I didn't realize my day-to-day existence was going to change drastically.

A Terrible Shock

Bob was drinking pretty heavy. I found out by accident that he was going out with another woman. It came as a terrible shock so Bob moved out to the Timberline Hotel where he had a barbershop. I remember the kids crying at night, "Why doesn't Daddy come home?" The worst came — Bob couldn't keep up with the payments on the house, so we had to get out.

The folks came up and packed everything as I landed in the hospital, and at 7:00 a.m., June 18, 1961, Ellen Rose Long was born. Sometimes in the hospital I would have a bath and by myself I cried and cried. I was at a terrible point of despair, a new baby, lost my home . . .

I prayed for help.

"I got sick with a high fever and a neighbour man took me to the hospital. The next day, I remember seeing Dad walking down the hallway of the hospital, where he was coming to cut patients' hair. He was shocked to see me in the hospital. I realize now that he hadn't been home the night before."

Linda

"One night that Dad came in and headed straight for the money jar in the kitchen. That was Mom's education fund that she had started for us kids. I remember her saying "No! No!" But he took it anyway, to buy drinks I guess."

Cathy

Opposite page:
(top) Linda's Sunday school class, see far right, June 1961

(middle) Linda, age 4 or 5

(bottom) Linda, dressed up for Hinton parade, 1960

This page:
Linda graduating from kindergarten, 1960

4

Settling and Unsettling: Thorsby — 1961-1965

When Bob came in to see me in the hospital, he said he was sorry and asked if we could try again. Here we go again! Well, at the time I did not have a choice. I told Bob that the only way it could work was if we moved away from Hinton. So Bob got a job in Thorsby working in a pool hall and a barbershop and rented a small house beside the United Church. Before I was able to leave the Hinton Hospital I developed a blood clot in my leg. Bob took Cathy (age nine) and Linda (age seven) and moved to Thorsby. By this time, we had sent Ronnie Veres back to live with his own family. When the doctor let me out of the hospital, I went with the new baby and Ida (age three) and stayed two or three weeks with the Harstones. They were so good

"I remember getting put into the back of a camper truck at night with Cathy and feeling excited about going for a ride. I woke up in a strange town with my dad and my sister. We went to an old house and Dad told us this was our new home. I hadn't known we were moving."

Linda

Opposite page:
Cathy (approaching 13) Ellen(2) Ida (approaching 6) Linda (9) Thorsby, 1963

This page:
Cathy's 10th birthday, left to right: Linda (7) Ida (4) Cathy and neighbours Shirley Voden and Joanne Connally

"She was going through a very difficult time and yet she maintained her faith. She loved life. That's one thing. She had a big ability to forgive. It's a gift from God that makes life a lot more pleasant."

Jean Harstone, 73, a neighbour from Hinton who helped Mary during a difficult time

"I remember living in this mansion of a house in Thorsby. I was so impressed at the time but when I went to visit it last year, it had shrunk."

Ida, Mary's daughter

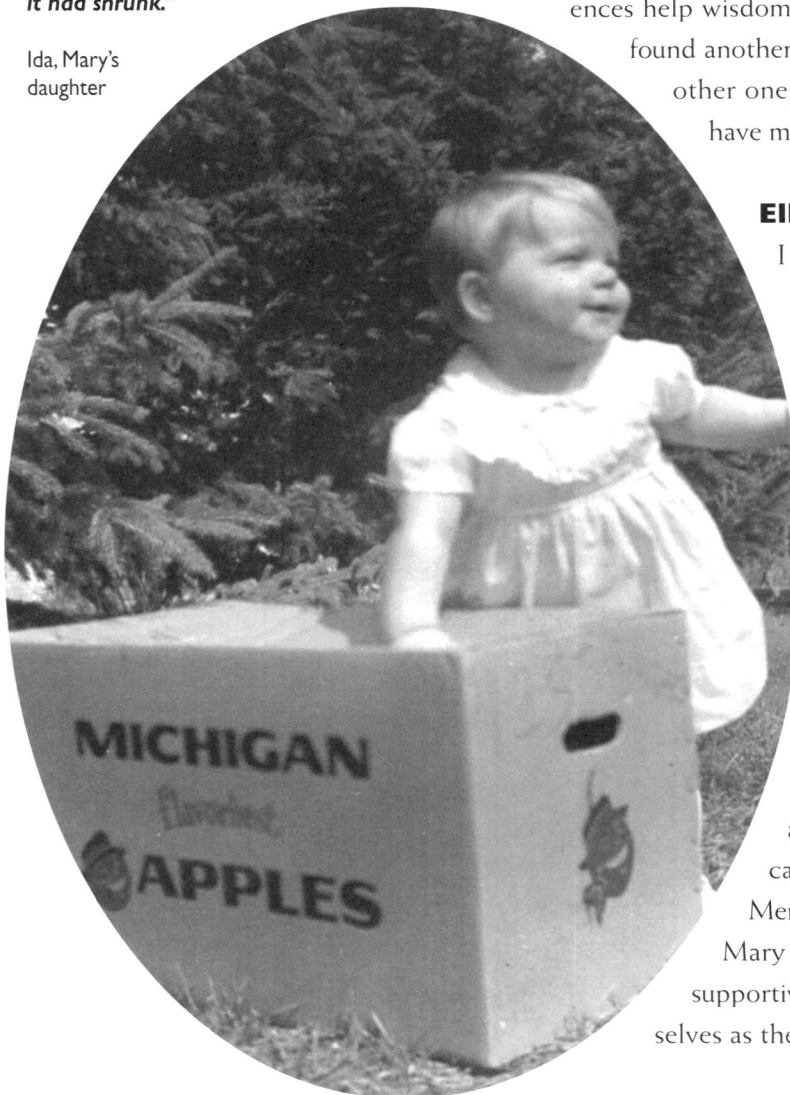

to Ida and me. They called Ida their princess. They were surely our guardian angels at this tragic time in our lives.

When I arrived in Thorsby, things were still a mess and not settled at all. I remember sitting on boxes with a new baby in my arms and crying. It was hard moving into this small house after having such a nice home in Hinton. There is much to forgive in this life, therefore wisdom develops. Believe you me, we are not born with wisdom — life's many experiences help wisdom to come. Guess what? We are moving again! We found another house in Thorsby. It wasn't much bigger than the other one, but it was nicer. Are you counting the times we have moved? So far, I believe it's 12.

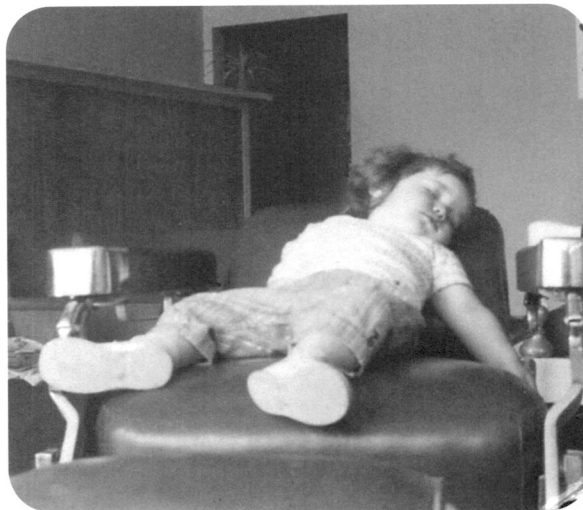

Ellen Rose

I was 33 years old when Ellen was born. She was a lovely baby, chubby and happy. She was also big at birth, weighing in at nine pounds, six ounces. She had medium-brown hair. God blessed me with another beautiful baby. One thing about Ellen, she loved eating beet pickles! We have a home movie of her asleep on the kitchen table with beet juice running down her face.

Home, Family and Community

We had a big yard where I could grow a big garden. I did a lot of canning and freezing vegetables, and sewing clothes to help the budget. Ken and Mary moved to Thorsby, and Mary and I became great friends. I don't know how it came about, but Bob's sister Eileen and her husband Mervin moved to Thorsby too. One big happy family! Mary was always someone I could talk to and she was supportive of me through trying times. We referred to ourselves as the out-laws, not the in-laws!

One day at our meal table, we were having fish, and Ida exclaimed, "Don't buy this anymore — there's too many thistles in it." One time in grade one or two, Ida went to school on Halloween dressed as a clown, only to find out that no one else was dressed up. She got very upset and ran crying to the washroom where she tried to wash all the paint off. Ida was always a deeply sensitive child.

I remember another day Linda was out on the swing; she came in and said, "I swung so high I touched the sky and I saw God." One time when we were in church, there wasn't room for us to sit all together. Linda had to sit several pews ahead of me and I wasn't in a position where I could stop her as she started taking off her shoes and socks! So, I just had to sit quietly and hope for the best. First, she very slowly took off one shoe at a time and placed each one carefully in front of her. Then she took off each sock, shook it, and carefully placed it over her shoes. Finally, she sat there pulling up and down on her hat, which had an elastic under the chin. Then she put her shoes and socks back on. She never made a sound. She just did all these things methodically. I think everyone was watching Linda, instead of listening to the sermon. When Linda graduated from kindergarten in Hinton, she wore a small graduation hat. This was a sign of things to come, when she graduated from university as a lawyer.

I remember that Cathy went in the Thorsby parade with her bicycle all decorated and a bride doll in her basket. Cathy always liked beautiful things and it was not surprising that she became an artist later.

While we lived in Thorsby, I went to Missouri by train with Ken and Mary to visit relatives. When we were there, I had a gallbladder attack and landed in Boon County Hospital for two days. Before I left

"I remember feeling that I had seen God that day on the swing. I was seven. I had absolute freedom and safety in Thorsby. Those were my happiest years."

Linda

Opposite page:
(top) Ida (age 3) sleeping in the barber chair where Bob worked, 1961

(bottom) Ellen Rose (about 1 year), 1962

This page:
(top) With my four girls and neighbour Joanne Connally (left), 1962

(middle) Ida (age 6), grade 1, 1963

Cathy (age 11) grade 6, 1962

(bottom) Linda (age 10), grade 4, 1964

"I was so happy because I won first prize in the bicycle division."

Cathy.

Opposite page:
*Cathy in the Thorsby parade,
1962*

*(left) Cathy (age 12),
grade 7, 1963*

This page:
*Cathy (14) made these
matching blue and white
outfits for herself and Ellen (4)
in Thorsby, 1965*

"One of us kids always used to take Dad his supper at the barbershop. This was a great privilege, as whoever took it always got a little treat. I was always happy when it was my turn!"

Ida

"Opening up the Snack Bar was a really big deal. It was something we were all very proud of. We were in the eye of the community. I remember Mom being really excited — it gave her a chance to get out more into the community and be social, which she's so good at. We were the first restaurant in town to introduce trendy junk foods like deep-fried chicken and we were the only place with soft ice cream. The Snack Bar is still in Thorsby."

Cathy

"No matter what it was, she could find something funny in it."

Frankie (Mary), 72.

Opposite page:
(left) Cathy (age 13), grade 8

(right) Linda (age 12) grade 7

This page:
(top) My girls (11, 8, 5, and 1) with Joanne Connally, 1962

(middle) Ida (age 7), grade 2, 1964

(bottom) Linda (age 9), grade 3, 1963

Thorsby, Bob had given me $200 spending money. Turns out, I had to spend it on the hospital and wire home for more. Well, I didn't shop and couldn't eat hardly any of the wonderful Missourian food. After coming back from Missouri in April, I had my gallbladder out in June. Ellen was still very small.

Thorsby was a farming community that was predominantly Ukrainian. I don't remember participating in many things in the community. When you've got a young family like I did, your whole world revolves around them, getting them off to school and everything. The Connallys lived across the street — they were also musical so we had some parties with singing and dancing. There was another neighbour named Stanley Ruff — he and his wife would come over. He was 6'5". I couldn't dance with him worth a hoot. He was too tall!

In 1962 or 1963, Bob decided to start up his own business — a snack bar with a barbershop in the same building. The business

was a chicken franchise, plus we sold ice cream and hamburgers. I made the girls and myself matching yellow and white, checked dresses to celebrate the grand opening of the Snack Bar.

Packing Up and Leaving

In 1965, I knew I was pregnant with David. My marriage was on the rocks. I decided I'd had enough of the drinking, other women, and verbal abuse. So approximately two months before the birth of David, I phoned a truck company, and the kids and I packed up, loaded and left.

"I was upset that we couldn't take my sandbox. Ida comforted me by explaining that we could get another one."

Ellen

Pizza Plenty: Eat in or Take Out. We ran the pizza shop In Leduc from 1967 to 1971.

5

Trying Years, Deepening Faith: Leduc — 1965 to 1971

I rented a house in Leduc and went to a lawyer who helped me get established on welfare. This lawyer was free through the United Church, otherwise I could not have managed financially. The place we rented was a two-storey house beside the United Church. It was the old manse that belonged to the church. It was pretty drafty and unevenly heated because it only had one source of heat — a floor furnace in the dining-room, living-room part. We paid $65 a month for rent.

David Tracy

So this is where I brought the new baby boy, David Tracy Long, who was born at 2:00 a.m. on October 17, 1965 in the Leduc hospital. David weighed nine pounds and eight ounces and he had dark hair. Finally after four girls, a boy! When David was born, Cathy was 14 years old, Linda was 11, Ida was eight and Ellen was four. I was 37 at the time of David's birth. We all loved this new baby and spoiled him proper.

The hospital wouldn't let the girls visit me, so the woman who was watching them brought them to the outside window of my room. I can still see their four little noses pressed against the window. When I came home, the girls were so proud of him, they couldn't get

"I waited anxiously for our bicycles to come off the moving truck because I couldn't wait to see what it felt like to ride on a paved road for the first time. The transition from gravel to pavement was a high. It was like gliding on ice."

Ida

"It was hard and we were poor but I was glad we were away from Dad."

Cathy

Opposite page:
My 1959 Nash Rambler, decorated for the Leduc parade, 1967

This page:
David Tracy, age 6 or 7 months, behind our house in Leduc, 1966. David loved playing in his Jolly Jumper

"I remember standing outside the hospital window. I had prayed for a boy and David was the answer to my prayer."

Linda

"I've often heard how little we had while growing up. Somehow, at the time, it didn't seem we lacked anything and, even now, I know that the abundance of possessions does not constitute the quality of one's life."

David

"I incinerated my eyebrows and eyelashes while trying to cook on the Coleman camp stove! I remember pouring snow taffy into the snow drifts that collected in the back porch of our house."

Linda

"A few years ago, I found Mom's budget book from our early years in Leduc. Every penny was recorded. Alongside the costs of food and rent was an entry for David's first baby booties, time-payments on a tricycle for me, meagre allowances for Cathy, Linda and Ida and, without fail, a weekly church offering of 10 cents."

Ellen

This page:
Linda (age 12), grade 7, 1966

enough of holding him. I couldn't believe the gifts I received. I hardly had to buy a thing. My faith in God at this time was not very strong but now, when I look back, our every need was looked after and I really didn't have to worry about anything.

Cooking on a Coleman Camp Stove

Upon settling in, I discovered the house was not wired for my electric stove. There was nothing to do but set up our Coleman camp stove in the kitchen. This is what I used to cook and to sterilize baby bottles. On Sunday, for a treat, I would buy a cheap cake mix, put a few slices of pineapple in the cast-iron frying pan, put the cake mix in, then put a lid on it. When it was cooked, I turned it out on a plate and we had lovely pineapple upside-down cake for Sunday dinner. I couldn't leave the baby so every week it was Linda's job to go uptown and buy a gallon of high-test gas for cooking. It cost 50 cents. We ate macaroni many times before the welfare cheque came. I might say here that we used that camp stove for 10 months. That was a hard winter for us.

My sister Francis heard of my plight and shipped me a gas stove from the farm. It had been stored in a granary and the mice ate the insides out so I couldn't use it. After that I would be sitting alone in the evening and pretty soon I had company. Scampering across the floor were two or three mice, small with large ears and pointed noses. I think they're called shrews and I'm sure they came from that old stove.

The Reverend Stewart Munro and his family lived across the street and when they found out I didn't have a stove, well, we never went without cakes or cookies after that. Half of Helen Munro's baking came over to our table. It was Reverend Munro who baptized David. When the water was sprinkled on David's head, he kicked so hard, he left his blue booties on the altar. David was always an active child. I remember one time, he pulled the legs off some daddy-long-legs and he ate the bodies. By evening, he was all puffed up!

One time, Ida was invited with the Munros to go on a TV show called *Popcorn Playhouse*. When the host asked Ida how old she was, she said, "I am eight and three-quarters years old." When Ida was in the younger grades, I taught her to crochet a simple chain stitch. Well, she crocheted five or so feet, and took it to school in a brown paper bag to show and tell.

My, What a Christmas

That first Christmas I wondered how I would manage to buy gifts. I needn't have worried. On Christmas Eve, a Santa Claus from Santa's Anonymous came and, wouldn't you know, a few minutes after that, Bob showed up with a bunch of toys. I was already very embarrassed that Bob arrived at the same time as Santa's Anonymous. As if that wasn't bad enough, then the Chamber of Commerce shows up with food, canned goods and much more. My cupboards were overflowing. My, what a Christmas. My faith was weak in those days, but after that it became considerably stronger.

One Last Chance for Bob

In the spring of 1967, Bob wanted to come back, so after several weeks of counselling, we decided to try again. He told me he would go to Alcoholics Anonymous and I decided I would go to Al-Anon. I thought Bob was really trying to straighten out his life. He went to work under another barber in Leduc at a place called Harry's. One cold winter day, while Bob was cutting hair, someone ran in and said, "A little boy has his tongue stuck on a fire hydrant, do you have some warm water?" So Bob went out to help and exclaimed, "That's not a boy, that's Linda!" It was Linda, not going anywhere, for sure. Bob used to give her such terrible short haircuts — I guess she looked like a boy stuck on that fire hydrant.

During that same winter, Cathy and her friend Dorothy Seidel got into some alcohol. Not realizing what they were doing, they drank too much and Cathy passed out in a back alley. It was a cold winter's night and she nearly froze to death before someone found her.

"My first memory of Christmas was the year that Santa's Anonymous came to our house. I felt very special that Santa Claus himself had paid a visit. I felt a big sense of relief—I had been worried that Santa wouldn't know where we were living."

Ellen (four at the time)

"I didn't believe in Santa anymore, but I was overjoyed with the gift that I got. It was a doll with a red velvet dress. The neighbour kids didn't see that it was anything special, but this didn't change how I felt."

Ida (nine at the time)

"I felt humiliated. I could see that Santa was the manager of our local grocery store and the father of one of my best friends. I never played with my friend again after that."

Linda (11 at the time)

"I was deeply embarrassed when Santa's Anonymous arrived. The kids were so delighted, but I was humiliated.

Cathy (14 at the time)

This page:
One last chance for Bob. Our ages from oldest to youngest: 41, 39, 16, 13, 10, 6 and about 9 months, early summer 1966

Working at Blunts' Nursing Home

To help with the bills, I went out to work at Blunts' Nursing Home where I received $1.65 an hour. I did shift work. It seemed that patients always died on the night shift. I was taught how to prepare the bodies. One time I helped prepare a body and then put a sheet up over the man's face. When the doctor came in he lifted the sheet and said, "I *hope* he's dead!" The next time, I waited for the doctor to put the sheet over the person's face. Another time I was feeding a patient dinner and he expired on the last bite. No wonder I lost 20 pounds within the first two months of working at that job.

Working at Blunts' was one of the hardest experiences I ever had, yet it was one of the best in many ways. I became very fond of the helpless old people. It was an eye-opener, because many of the residents had hardly any visitors and we staff became like their family. And yet we were so busy we couldn't spend much time with each person. I remember one Ukrainian woman couldn't speak a word of English. She jabbered at us verbally as well as with her fists. She was a big woman of about 250 pounds. One night, two of us were trying to put this woman to bed and both of us went home from that shift with black and blue bruises. She was finally moved to another hospital.

There was this one very elderly man who needed a lot of help. The first time I took him to the bathroom, be danged if he didn't try to put his hand up my skirt. Well, he was old enough to know better. There's no fool like an old fool! I guess he wasn't all there. Anyway, I asked not to care for him after that.

At the time, I had a red-headed babysitter who lived with us. I can't remember her name. I worked at Blunts' nearly a year, then I had to quit when this babysitter didn't work. I had to let her go because she was more interested in her boyfriend than in the proper care of my children. About this time, the idea of opening a pizza shop was in the works. In 1967, we opened "Pizza Plenty" on the main street of Leduc.

Our Trip to Missouri

Before we opened the pizza shop, we travelled by car to Missouri to visit Bob's relatives. David stayed with the Munros. One time, when we were on the road, we pulled over to answer the call of nature. I was doing my business,

while hiding between two open car doors. For a joke, Bob quickly closed the back door and drove away, leaving me hanging in mid-air, much to my consternation.

We brought back a turtle that we called Little Moe, in a tea kettle that was stacked with other things on the roof of the car. We drilled a little hole in the edge of Moe's shell so he could be put on a chain. That way, he could be outside and not escape. One time, he got unhooked and went clear across the road. We eventually gave him to Story Land Valley Zoo in Edmonton.

Opening the Pizza Shop, Losing Cathy

After a year and a few months, our marriage broke up again. I would not be so unkind as to put the reasons on paper. Anyway, I was left to run the pizza shop by myself. Earl Krussert of Edmonton had backed Bob in this venture — I ended up making payments to him after Bob left. Things were pretty bad, with a big grocery bill rung up at the store and rent on the house being behind.

Cathy went to help her dad open another pizza shop in Lacombe and St. Albert. Neither place made it and Cathy joined the hippies and hitch-hiked to Montreal. I remember her coming home with bags and pots and pans hanging all over her. In the sixties many young people joined the hippie movement, much to the distress of parents. Alcoholism so devastating on children.

While still living in the old manse by the church I was going every day to the pizza shop. Linda was 13 or 14 years old and had a terrible amount of responsibility for a young girl. She worked in the shop, then had to look after Ellen, Ida and David at home. This was such a busy time for me and the children. It was difficult having the children at home while I was trying to run this shop too. I would work till

"When Dad pulled away leaving Mom exposed to the world, I laughed, but I remember not really feeling good about it. On the trip back from Missouri, the older girls tormented me by saying that mohair sweaters were made by tearing the shells off turtles like our Little Moe and collecting the hair that was underneath."

Ellen

"The pizza shop in Lacombe was a combination restaurant-gas station that was open 24 hours a day. It had a staff of eight and I ran the place by myself. Dad was running the pizza shop in St. Albert and he used to run supplies down to me once a week. After three months, it got too much for me, and I left for Montreal. I was 17 years old."

Cathy

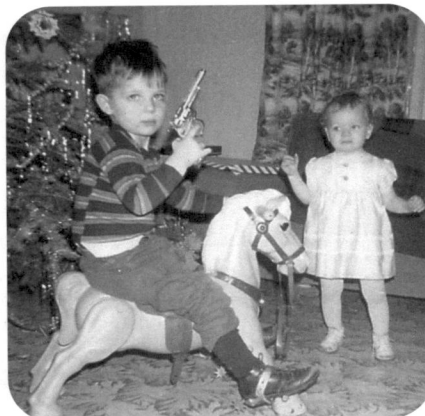

Opposite page:

(top) Age 39

(middle & bottom) David and I, winter 1966-1967

This page:

(top) David (approaching 2) with one of Bob's famed haircuts, summer 1967

(middle) Cathy (age 16), 1966

(bottom) David (age 26 months), and a cousin, Christmas 1967

"I worked 40 hours a week in the pizza shop and another 30 hours looking after my sisters and brother at home. I was in grade eight and nine. I remember our family blowing to bits with the stress of the pizza shop. I always forgave my mother; it was never her fault. She had absolutely no other choice. But I suffered with the decision.

Linda

"My dearest Ellen, You have not heard from me for a few days. For one thing, writing down some of these things brought all the emotions to the top again. I found it hard, so I quit for awhile. Just now I went out and bought a new writing pad. I am ready to have a go at it again."

Mary, in a note to Ellen about this book, 1998

Opposite page:
(top) Ida (age 12), grade 7, 1969

(bottom) Ida (age 11), grade 6, 1968

This page:
(top) Ellen (age 6), grade 1, 1967

(middle) Ellen (age 7), grade 2, 1968

(bottom) Ellen (age 8), grade 3, 1969

2:00 a.m. and then walk down the middle of the road by myself with all the money I had made that day under my coat. I was afraid of being robbed.

Losing Linda

To get back to Linda, I decided, and I have regrets about my decision, to send her to her dad's for what was supposed to be a few weeks. She was close to 15, and my thought at the time was that it would be a break for her from the stressful conditions and too much responsibility. I wasn't thinking about it in the long-term. But she ended up staying there. I can't remember all the reasons why she stayed. The effects of this decision lasted a lifetime and I wish things could have been different. I hope she really forgives me and has no doubts about my motives. Cathy joined the hippies. I lost two of my girls. This is what happens when a parent has a drinking problem. The kids suffer. It seems to leave them with a lifetime of scars and emotions to deal with. Life is very difficult sometimes.

At least one thing I have to be thankful for is that I wasn't a battered wife, and heaven knows there are lots of them in our society. One thing I know for sure, had I stayed with Bob, I would have lost my mind. I never should have taken him back after Thorsby but you don't know these things at the time. You always hope things will get better and there will be solutions to all problems.

Moving Into the Pizza Shop

I hired a young chap, but when I found out he was treating his friends for free, he got fired. Finally it was just too much, so I moved my family to two very small rooms in the back of the pizza shop. This was in 1968. David would've been about three; Ellen, seven; and Ida, 11. Ida slept in the basement which was really just an underground garage, and David, Ellen and I slept in one room upstairs. The second upstairs room was really for storage. We didn't have a bathtub. I don't remember how we bathed. We used the same washroom as the public. I guess we bathed in a wash tub. Sometimes now, when I hear some of the old songs from the sixties like "Bridge Over Troubled Water," it triggers old memo-

ries about the pizza shop. I really remember a song called "Imagine" and another called "Let it Be." When we lived there, we sure ate a lot of pizzas, hamburgers, hotdogs and French fries. We also sold homemade chocolate-covered bananas on a stick and shrimp chips. I also made corn dogs, which were hotdogs on a stick, deep-fried in batter. All of these things were quite popular with the teens.

One thing I remember while living in the pizza shop was attending at the birth of my niece Colleen's first baby (Shauna). That was a *really* neat experience. Even if I did lose a night's sleep, and had to run the pizza shop the next day, it was well worth it.

The Basement Floods

Shortly after we moved to the pizza shop, a cloudburst flooded the underground garage where a lot of my stuff was in boxes and mattresses were on the floor. A foot of water rushed down the driveway and everything I had was floating. All we could do was put the mattresses and bedding on fences to dry. A lot of our stuff was destroyed.

The Ups and Downs of a Teenage Clientele

At this time I owned a blue 1959 Rambler. Every week, I would back it out of the underground garage and drive to south Edmonton for wholesale supplies, including pizza crusts from the Pizza Plenty wholesale outlet. A lot of my sales were for takeout pizza.

The teenagers loved to come to my shop. I want to say that, for the most part, my experience with the teenagers of Leduc was positive. Of course, I had trouble with a handful of them. Once, when I was having some problems with two or three boys, I finally had to get the police in and lay charges and a few weeks later they came and apologized. They were sneaking alcohol into the business and storing empty bottles in the back of the toilet. On a less serious note, one boy took a plastic ketchup bottle and squeezed as fast and hard as he could. Consequently, I had a big streak of red ketchup on my ceiling and I could never get up there to clean it.

During my time at the pizza shop I didn't have much recreation but one winter I did take some square dance lessons. We did have some good times in that pizza shop. For a short time, on Saturday nights, we used to have hootenannies. I used to hire a small band to play in the front bay window. They always played "Rambling Rose" for me because I had a 1959 Nash Rambler. These events were real popular. The place

"There was a bathtub down in the basement, but it was just an old relic that wasn't hooked to anything. It was sitting in a wide-open space by the hot water heater. This one time, I hauled down pails of water from the upstairs bathroom sink. I only did it once because I was too nervous of someone opening the garage door or coming down the stairs."

Ida

"I love Auntie Joe very much. She's always been there for me.

Colleen, 47, daughter of Ken and Mary

"I never got used to sleeping down in that basement. I opened my eyes one morning to be greeted by a large, very majestic-looking daddy-long-legs, sitting on my chest, staring at me. That was it! I moved a mattress upstairs into a long, narrow storage space. The single mattress just fit with the edges curling a bit on each side."

Ida

"I remember being home for Thanksgiving dinner, and seeing Mom cut a turkey up into pieces that would fit into the pizza oven. Even though she didn't have a proper home, she had not lost her traditions."

Linda

A Few Words from the Pizza Shop Teenagers

I was just going into puberty when the pizza shop opened and it was there for five years. Mrs Long (Mary) gave us a place. She accepted us. It made me feel like she really cared about us, the young people. I think it mattered to her that we were safe, that we had a place to go.

I definitely admired her, and her guts. She's a pretty amazing lady, I'll tell you. She has a special gift. I knew she had a long, hard road, but she still had a smile for us. She'd try to get us to look at both sides of things. Try to get us to understand what our parents might be thinking. She counselled us. She touched a lot of people's lives and influenced how they thought about things.

When she left the pizza shop, nobody went there anymore. She had always made a point to talk to people who were sitting alone. It didn't matter whether they were young or old. My mom had coffee with her a lot. When she (Mary) left, the warm inviting atmosphere was gone.

In all these years, I've never forgotten her. And it's not just us teenagers who will remember. Our children will too, because the pizza shop was part of our youth, and we talk to our kids about that. I've told my own daughter a lot of stories about (Mary) and the pizza shop. I'm even writing about it in the memory book that I'm keeping for my granddaughter. I think Mary must be a bit of a legend in Leduc.

**Bernadette (Lamanas) Brodie,
now 42 years of age**

More Words from the Pizza Shop Teenagers

*The whole place would be full of these loud, rowdy hippies.
She'd just lean over the counter and very quietly say, "Now you kids, pipe down."
And that'd be it, the whole place would quiet down. They knew they
were in the presence of someone special.
They respected her.*

*A lot of kids would go to her. She didn't judge. She was an example
of strength and wisdom. Whenever a chaotic situation arose
that a lot of parents would have freaked out about, she would stay calm
and just say one line that would resonate deeply inside.
It taught me respect.*

*She came for coffee last year in a restaurant I was working in it was like
seeing Mother Mary! I knew her when I was between 12 and 17 years old. She
had a very strong impact on my life. She became a huge part of me. No
matter how bleak things got, she could alway come up with a solution and
live it immediately. She has unbelievable faith and fortitude. I learned
about living life on life's terms by observing her.*

**Julia Mae Malec,
now 43 years of age**

"I remember having to work a lot at lunchtime, after school and every weekend. It got to me."

Ida

"The hootenannies Mom held in the pizza shop were one of the highlights of my childhood! I loved to see Mom singing and enjoying herself."

Ellen

"One of my most vivid memories of the pizza shop was when a band of my long-haired friends came dressed in tails and tuxedos and played in the front window. One of the players accidentally broke the overhead light with the neck of his mandolin."

Cathy

"She was very good at drawing people out of themselves and offering sparing, careful advice, not mentioning all the while any of her own dilemmas or concerns."

Ellen

"I remember Mom calmly listening to the drug-withdrawal confessions of a local teenager. She was always there for young people."

Linda

was always jam-packed with teenagers who came to sing along. I liked those kids.

Because the teenagers liked to come to my place, some parents thought I was giving drugs to the kids. One Saturday night, a policeman sat near where I was cooking the pizza and watched my every move. The next Saturday, he came again and this time, he came right around the counter and looked in everything. How do you think I felt? I went on Monday morning to the police station and gave them a piece of my mind. After that they left me alone. I remember one Saturday night my landlord was peering in the back window and scared the living daylights out of my kids. Boy what did he think, I was running an illicit operation in the back? I didn't like him a bit.

In contrast to the teenagers who came to the pizza shop, two elderly brothers by the name of McLaren used to come in everyday for lunch. I don't think they liked pizza all that much, but they wanted to support my business. They ran a law office a block away. Sometimes they would get David or Ellen to deliver lunches or dinners to their office. They always gave a tip of a quarter, which was a lot at the time. Later, I got these kindly gentlemen to do some legal work for me and they gave me a real break on the price.

When you're serving the public, you have to put up with a lot and you never know what to expect. One Saturday night, I accidentally spilled a cup of hot coffee in a customer's lap. He was so polite about it. Later the same night, I ran out of little creams for the coffee so I served canned milk. Boy, this one customer dressed me up one side and down the other. I was totally subdued by the time he got finished with me. This was not one of my better nights.

Welcome Companionship

One day a big man with nice brown eyes came in and introduced himself as Mr. Billsborrow. After a time he ask me and the children to go on a picnic. Well, Ed was just what I needed at the time. He provided friendship, fixed my car, and in general he was very supportive. Although we never had a serious relationship, we were going together for about two years. Sometimes we would go on picnics and spend time out at his farm. Even when I moved to Nisku he came to visit. One thing I remember about Ed was that he couldn't laugh out loud. He had some funny sayings like "My mother's moustache" and "South African pig bristles," but all the time I knew him he never swore. Just an all-around good man.

"I remember driving Mr. Billsborrow's tractor all over his farm. Also, he was the one who took me out on the gravel roads to teach me how to drive a car."

Ida

"I was sick with worry when Mom took a second job."

Ellen

"It was crazy with Mom on her feet 12 to 14 hours a day and the family living in the back."

Cathy

The Breaking Point

Finally, after five years of the pizza shop, I was played out. I just barely managed to keep my head above water the whole time. It was a hand-to-mouth existence and then things were starting to go downhill. For awhile, I tried making extra money by taking a second job in the mornings before the pizza shop opened at noon. I worked on an assembly line putting toppings on pizzas at the Pizza Plenty wholesale outlet. I couldn't hack that for long. More standing on my feet.

I wasn't doing a good job of being a businesswoman and mother and father to my precious kids. One memory I have was threatening to send my kids to an orphanage if they didn't behave. David was really young and being raised on Main Street was less than desirable. I realized this when someone came in and told me David was roof-hopping from one business to another, and also tried to fill a window-well with water so he could swim. The last straw was when he broke some windows in a doctor's clinic and I had to pay the bill.

I remember Ellen landing in the hospital with a terrible cough. They never found what was causing it and I won-

Opposite page:
(top) David (age 6), grade 1, 1971

(middle) Ida (age 10), grade 5, 1967

(bottom) With a cute little garden imp, bottom left

This page:
(top) Mr. Billsborrow with Ida (12), Ellen (8) and David (4), at Muttart Conservatory, Edmonton.

(middle) Talking on the phone in the pizza shop, age 42, 1970

(bottom) Ellen (age 9), grade 4, 1970

"When I was six years old, I turned on the outside water faucet that was over top of the basement window-well at the Leduc post office. My intention was to let it fill up with water while I ran home for my swimsuit so I could return for a dip. When I came back, I encountered a very mad postmaster who dragged me inside and held me over top of a very large mail bag and threatened to send me to Tibet should I ever do that again!"

David

"I shudder to think about what would have happened if we hadn't been able to get out of that pizza shop. In our final year there, Ida tried to drop out of grade nine, David failed grade one, and I should have failed grade five, but my teacher passed me along because he knew the situation."

Ellen

"The school told us they would fine Mom $500 if I dropped out because I was underage. For that reason, I went back because I knew she couldn't afford that fine."

Ida

"Mom threw a big surprise party for me on my 10th birthday. I don't know how she managed it, working up front and running this kids' party in the back. I was thrilled."

Ellen

dered if it was the stress of our situation. My kids missed out on a lot of one-on-one attention. I just worked all the time. The responsibility of the pizza shop was too much for Ida also.

Touched by God's Love

I put the pizza shop up for sale but no one seemed interested in buying it. I was in a pit of despair. I was thinking about shutting it down and just walking away. One day, when I was cleaning the shop, I saw something on the floor. I picked it up. On one side, I saw a picture of a robin and it said, "Your Father Careth for You" from *The Book of Matthews*. Then I turned it over and it was a mirror. I had a wonderful feeling come over me and I felt I was again touched by God's love. Shortly after that, the shop sold!

An Italian fellow came in and wanted to see my books. The next day his whole family came and watched while I served my customers. They decided to buy, giving me two weeks to get out. I got $10,000 for the business. Now I was in a dilemma. Business sold and no place to live. By then, Cathy had moved back to Leduc and rented an apartment above the movie theatre. Two or three days after the business sold, Cathy's boyfriend, Ron Kingsbury, came in and said he knew of some people in Nisku who were selling their house. I closed shop that same afternoon and went to see the house.

The Dwyers were asking $14,000 for their house. At this point in my life I really prayed and asked God for the other $4,000. In talking to the Dwyers I told them I only had $10,000 and they said, "Well, get a lawyer, and we will take a second mortgage for you for $4,000."

Talk about my prayers being answered when my need was most desperate. So the business sold and a house was found within two weeks. Then I hit an unexpected problem.

The McLaren brothers were the ones I got to draw up the legal papers for the house. During the time I was having the papers done, I had to call

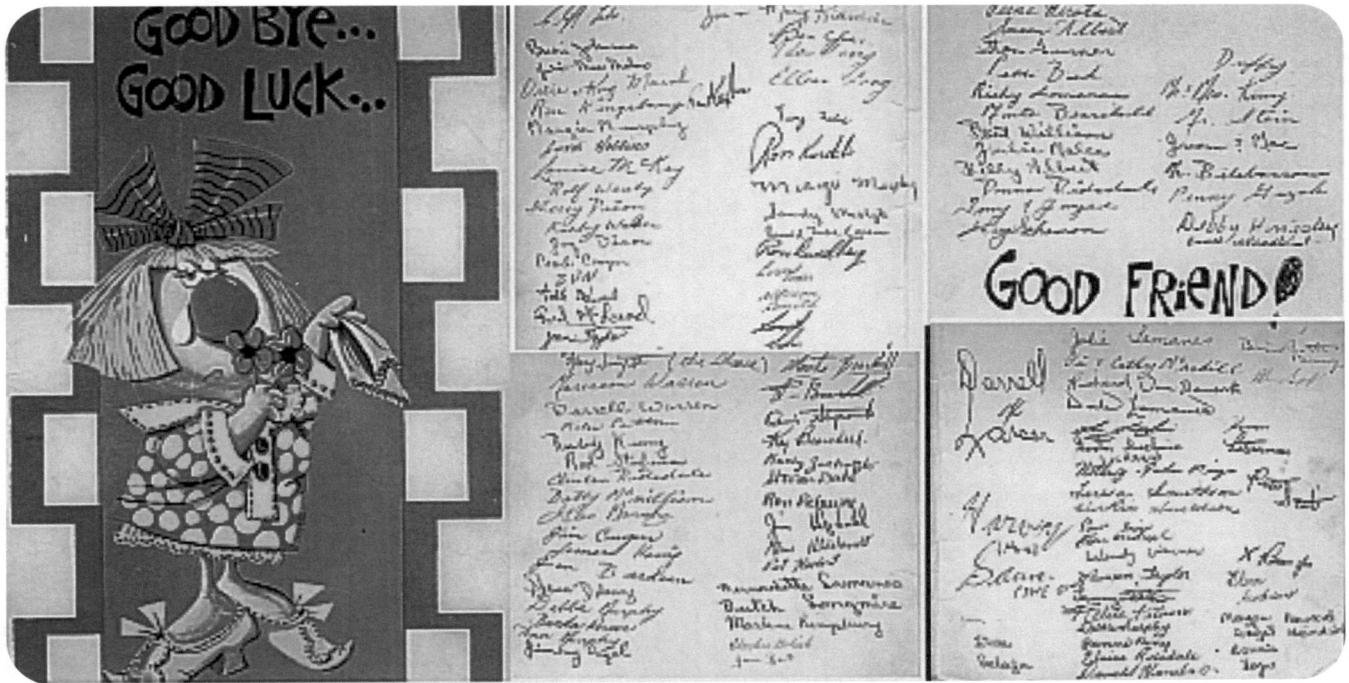

a government office in Wetaskiwin to get some information about something. I don't remember exactly what the information was that I needed but I discovered that because of Bob's unpaid debts, there was a legal judgment against him. Because we were still legally married, this judgment meant that I couldn't get the mortgage I needed to get the house in Nisku. I don't think I've ever told my kids about this. Anyway, I just kept praying. It came to pass that within a few days of being told about the judgment, the office that had the judgment papers accidentally lost them while moving to a new building. And so the sale of the house went through! Once again, I felt like God's hand was really guiding us.

Before we left Leduc, the teenagers from the pizza shop threw a big party for me and gave me gifts and a beautiful card. Some of those kids used to come visit me years later.

"I remember the day that Mom found that mirror. I shared in Mom's joy when God opened the doors to let the pizza shop go."

Ida

Opposite page:
(top) Ida (age 13), grade 8, 1970

(bottom) Ida (age 13), working in the pizza shop, 1970

This page:
(top) The teenagers from the pizza shop gave me this card in 1971.

(bottom) Ida (age 14), grade 9, 1971

6

New Beginnings:
Nisku — 1971 to 1984

Moving to Nisku was a memorable time for us. Nisku was a small hamlet of about 50 people. We had a house of our own with a garden. Although I had no money left over and we had to go on welfare for a time, I was happy because it felt like getting out of a prison to get that pizza shop sold. When we moved to Nisku, I was 43 years old; Ida, 14; Ellen, 10; and David, six.

The first day we moved in, I heard David in the back yard swearing, so I went out and paddled his bum. Then I came in and started to have a shower. Only cold water came out and I screamed from the shock. I guess I was at the end of my rope and, you poor kids, I took it out on you. This makes me cry even as I write about it. I said, and I quote, "What kind of people do you think the neighbours will think have moved in here — the little boy swearing in the back-yard and the mother screaming in the shower!" End of quote.

Freedom

The next day, while I was amid boxes, a neighbour woman, Muriel McConnell, came over to welcome us. I started making her some tea, when all of a sudden, "bump, bump, bump," David came roaring down the stairs on a piece of cardboard! Oh well, he was only six and the freedom we all felt in a 10-room house was wonderful after two small back rooms at the pizza shop. Ellen showed a great interest in music at this time and

"When I visited from Vancouver, I was overwhelmed to see the house at Nisku. I was so happy that Mom had something of her own."

Cathy

"Shortly after moving to Nisku, I started pumping gas at the local Turbo Station after school and on weekends waitressed at the Airway Motor Inn. It helped make ends meet."

Ida

"Nisku was a great place to grow up— a little bit country life and a little bit town life. I always had to keep my imagination working to stay entertained."

David

Opposite page:
Our new 10-room house was like a castle to us!

This page:
The view from our front door

"The piano was the first thing the movers brought into the house. I immediately sat down and started playing. As I listened to the sound echo throughout the big, wondrous space, I remember feeling like a tight band was being loosened from my chest."

Ellen

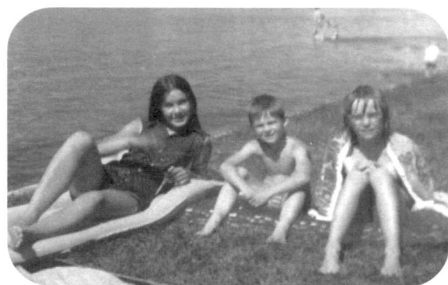

This page:

(top right) The piano that my mother bought in the 1930's

(top left) David (age 7), grade 1, 1972

(bottom left) Ida, David and Ellen on one of our adventures at the lake, 1971

(bottom right) David (age 7), Ellen (11) and Ida (15), 1972

played by ear on the old black piano. She was always very musical and still plays the piano and the accordion, and sings with several music groups.

Speaking of the pizza shop, I would like to say that it closed a year after I sold it. The man I sold it to had different ideas about running it than I did. I depended on the high school crowd and he drove them out. Consequently the business failed and he came to my door one day trying to sell me a vacuum cleaner. He was downright nasty, but it wasn't my fault he lost his business.

Camping Adventures

The first summer at Nisku was all one big adventure. We had an old tent and all we could afford for holidays was camping trips. We used to go to a lake north of Edmonton called Long Lake. The kids and I had campfires and sang songs in the evenings. Of course camping is no picnic as far as work is concerned (pun intended!). The children had a wonderful time. I can't remember if I had a good time or not, as I was very exhausted after these trips. Of course, to see the kids have a good time was worth it.

My, how I loved those kids. Sometimes I sweat blood and tears they did not see.

One weekend in July we decided to camp out at Joseph Lake only about a half-hour from home. On Saturday night we had a terrific thunderstorm. Wet and disappointed we made our way home early Sunday. When we got there, I happened to open the door to the basement, and what a shocking surprise — there was five feet of water! At Nisku the water table is very high, so at all times it was necessary to have a sump pump running in our basement. The sump pump was on a wall switch that had to be left in the on-position in order for it to kick in when the water got too high, which happened a lot in the summer time. Well, wouldn't you know, while we were away the gas meter man came, read the meter and turned the switch off.

No Hot Water and No Heat

I immediately put on the switch and it took six hours for the water to pump out. Our hot water heater was shot and the motor in the furnace was no good. Since I was still on welfare and, not knowing what else to do, I contacted the welfare office.

They offered to put in a hot water heater and ordered a furnace motor. It took a month or maybe more to get the hot water heater installed so I was heating a lot of water on the stove for baths and washing clothes.

Now the furnace motor was something else. It was ordered in July and I didn't get it until early November. The motor had to come from down East, and that summer there was a big train strike. We were suffering through an uncomfortable situation but, you know, where there's a will, there's a way. By fall we covered the kitchen doorways with blankets, and kept warm with the gas oven. Bedtime saw us dashing upstairs with fog from our breath around us and quickly getting our clothes off and crawling into cold sheets. I think we had a hot water bottle at the time which helped. When the motor arrived we basked in the luxury of a warm house again.

One of my experiences as a single mom was that I became very handy at fixing things. I had to, because I couldn't afford to hire anyone. When the iron went on the blink, I took it all apart and I got it working. Another project was fixing an electrical plug-in switch. I shut off the breaker, took everything apart, repaired the wire, and guess what? It worked! I got so I could do a lot of things: balance the budget, check the oil in the car, put air in the tires, and a lot of other things.

Linda moved back home for a very short time before she joined the military in the mid '70s. One Christmas when Linda was home, she was showing me some of the things she was learning in the military. We were play-wrestling and a vein ruptured in my groin. My whole stomach turned black and blue. As awful as this sounds, it really was quite funny at the time. The doctor ordered me off my feet for the rest of the Christmas holidays. Consequently, the kids had to put on the Christmas dinner!

"I remember bathing in a steel washtub in the living room on Friday nights. I think I was always the last one to use the water!"

David

"When we'd have to use the oven to cook supper, the room would get cold. We couldn't wait to get that oven door open again."

Ida

"Nisku was a palace and an entitlement. I never lived there, except for a couple of months after high school, but it was always my home."

Linda

This page:

(top right) Ida (age 15), grade 10, 1972

(top left) Ellen (age 11), grade 6, 1972

(middle left) Linda (age 16), grade 11, 1970

(middle right) Linda (age 17), grade 12, 1971

(bottom left) Linda (age 16 or 17)

(bottom right) Linda age (15 or 16)

"She was a big influence on my life. She took us into her house and exposed us to music and the arts. I was quite shy at the time and didn't want to do things in public like singing. She got me to sing and I ended up singing at my own wedding. That's part of why I wanted Mary to come to my wedding, because the singing started with her."

Marco Valentini, neighbour, age seven when we moved to Nisku

"She is still the one person who could talk me into anything."

Chinto Valentini, referring to the time he wore a dress and sang a Kitty Wells' song for a community Christmas concert

This page:
(top right) Ellen and Linda at the first community Christmas concert in Nisku, 1971

(bottom: from the left) Chris Garneau, David Long and Craig Bridge

Amanda and Gloria Garneau

Tammy Feldman and Joyce McConnell

Carlene Chisholm

Community Christmases and Community League

On balance, there were many joyous times in Nisku. Our Christmases were fun. Our first Christmas there, I had the energy then to place loudspeakers outside to play Christmas music and put lights and garlands all over the house. We decorated a nice Christmas tree and I could manage some decent presents.

Finally I thought, why not have a Christmas concert in my living room! I sent the word out, and the evening of the concert neighbours came and put long boards between chairs so a lot of people could sit. The living room and dining room were full of people. We had a wonderful time. The children sang "Let the Sunshine In, Face it with a Grin," recited poems, and put on a Nativity skit. Also, one girl did a ballet number and a boy, Chinto Valentini, put on my orange square dance dress, held a ukelele and pantomimed to a Kitty Wells' song. It was hilarious and received lots of hand clapping. The house was a shambles after this but it was all worth it. That was the best concert you ever could wish for, truly one of those memories worth preserving. It was great for a small community.

The next year, we moved to a large room at the Airways Hotel for our Christmas concert. Half an hour before I had to go on stage to emcee, I was brushing my false teeth and dropped them in the sink, breaking the front tooth. I just kept putting my hand over my mouth and wondered if I should sing "All I Want for Christmas is my *One Front Tooth.*"

Those teeth caused me problems at other

times too. Linda went to school in one of her younger grades and announced to the class that her mother just got "falsies." Good grief! One morning, I woke up and they were stuck on my bottom, leaving quite an impression for a while. Another time, I took a bite of a fresh-made bun, and out came my teeth sitting on top of the bun. Well, the kids thought this was hilarious.

During this time, I started a local community league to get activities for the children and make a sense of community. Nisku was missing something before that. People just slept there and went to their jobs. The community league gave more of a sense of community among the neighbours. We cleared rocks from a field and built a skating rink. Later, we made a winter carnival. Some of the young people made ice

sculptures. Rudy Garneau built a car out of ice, and spray-painted it. It was very good and won first prize. David dressed up in one of his sister's dresses stuffed with pillows and skated around the rink.

By this time, Cathy had already moved to Vancouver, where she went to art college and worked sewing costumes and dancing in the chorus line of a large nightclub. She also

This page:

(top) In 1972, we held the community Christmas concert at the Airways Hotel. Ellen (11) is in the back right with friend Elaine Woods

(bottom) Elaine Woods (left) was crowned Miss Nisku at the 1974 winter carnival; she's with Tammy and Joceline Garneau

"What always impressed me was she got the community meetings going with the women, making crafts and things. I was surprised that she could get everyone going like that. We were all pretty much newcomers in that area. People didn't get together much. She started the ball rolling."

Julie Valentini, neighbour

"She was quite a lady. She's got a good way with people."

Luigi Valentini, neighbour

"Your place was like a community drop-in centre. It didn't seem to matter what she was doing, she always made time when we came around. All the kids in the neighbourhood, we were always there. That was my second home there with you guys."

Chinto Valentini, age 10 when we moved to Nisku

"I loved it when my sisters would come home, Linda from the East and Cathy from the West. My exotic sisters from afar — I used to think of them as Carol Burnett and Cher!"

Ellen

sold a lot of her art work. At an early age, she showed artistic abilities. Later, she went on to make limited edition prints of Leduc's first oil well. One of these prints is in the Devon Historical Oil Museum and another is in the head office of Imperial Oil in Toronto. She has done many other artistic projects as well.

Starting to Work in the Fibreglass Plant

For about a year, I stayed home. Not many phone calls, just planting my garden and flowers. One day a woman named Bertha phoned up and asked if I might be able to babysit her children, Paul and Pam. Bertha deBoon and her husband, Huibert, were starting up a fibreglass business in Nisku Industrial Park. I babysat for her a few times, then one evening Huibert asked me if I would like to wax a houseboat mold. The aluminum mold was 12 feet wide by 36 feet long. I had to wax and polish it three times. When I was finished that, Huibert ask me if I would be interested in learning to be a fiberglasser. I decided to take on the challenge.

It was indeed an interesting challenge working with fibreglass. The first time I washed my dusty work clothes with the family wash was the last time I did so! Why, the next day, the kids came home and were going crazy with the itch. After that, I washed my clothes separate. I made houseboats to begin with. We made quite a sensation as a houseboat factory on the Prairies. In all we made 11 houseboats for Shuswap Lake in BC and many other things over the years. Anyway, I had a job and kept the house payments up and food on the table.

The Plant Burns Down

Eight months after the fibreglass business started, a terrible tragedy hit. On November 3, 1972, the business burned down along with the mobile home that Bertha and Huibert lived in with their children. The fire started at 6:00 in the morning in the office, which was attached to the mobile home. They think an electric heater was the cause. And of course fibreglass is very flammable. Bertha's brother was getting married the same day so Bertha's parents were visiting. They were sleeping on a hide-a-bed in the living room. They broke the big picture window and got out, suffering smoke inhalation and cuts from the glass. Bertha's brother, Willy, was sleeping in a houseboat in the shop. Fortunately, he managed to get out. Huibert and Bertha grabbed Pam and Paul and ran out into the snow and ice in their bare feet. It was a very frosty and cold night. Huibert and Bertha somehow got to the neighbour's to phone the fire department and I was also phoned for bandages. I drove to the neighbour's but they were all gone to the hospital by then. Bertha's parents were in the hospital for several days. We went around gathering clothes for them because everything

went up in smoke and fire. Bertha had canned around 400 jars of fruit in the fall and they had just put a bunch of beef in the deep freeze. They lost it all including the wedding gifts for that day.

What a thing! One day I had a job, the next day I had none. I wondered how I was going to provide for my family. I thought, "Oh no, back on welfare again."

Linda was in the armed forces at the time and she arrived home in the early morning of this fire. Seems if I remember right, we had a dog that scared her pretty bad. She used to come home a lot by surprise — this time, she got the surprise!

The Plant Gets Rebuilt

One week later Huibert deBoon walked into my kitchen and asked me if I would like to go to work again. I should mention that the business was under-insured. I think it was insured for $50,000 and they already put $80,000 into it. Well, it was enough to start building again. Some people would have given up but not the deBoons. Huibert had rented a bay at the back of the Nisku gas station and I went to work there making round marker balls that hang on power and telephone lines.

The menfolk put up a new building during 20° below (Fahrenheit) weather and every other kind of condition. I remember Huibert's brother Henry coming out from Edmonton to work on this building until his back gave out and he had to go into hospital for an operation. It was a successful operation. No more pain. I will never forget Huibert coming in one day, picking up a nail and saying, "You know, even this is so precious when you can't find any." It reminded me never to take for granted what we have and how important even the littlest things in life are.

A few weeks after Christmas, I moved over to the new shop and fibreglassed standing on rough dirt until the cement floors were poured. That dirt floor was the pits! My legs were never very good, and that made it worse. I decided to have my veins stripped in an operation. That put me out of commission for awhile.

Taking on Boarders and Finding Time to Socialize

This is about the time Carol Tylke came into the picture. She boarded at our house. Carol was a lovely girl. We went to Weight Watchers together. I lost 30 pounds in one year. Carol soon started in the fibreglass plant. Once she and I put three or four layers of fibreglass on this steel tank mold but when we came back in the morning the whole mess was on the ground. We had forgot to put the catalyst in the resin and so it didn't

"If all employees were like Mary, owning a business would be a dream."

Huibert deBoon, who hired Mary to work in the fibreglass shop.

"When I moved in, I was accepted right away. I'd never met anyone like Mary's kind. It's like she's some kind of angel-person. In all my years of meeting all kinds of people, there's nobody I've met better. There's no one like her in these parts. She's a true Christian."

Carol (Tylke) Rossiter, 45, boarded with us when she was in her late teens.

Opposite page:
David (age 8), grade 2, 1973

This page:
I'm wearing an outfit I made, shown here with Carol Tylke

harden. That, on top of everything else the business went through.

Another boarder we had was Julie Malec. Last year, I ran into her in a restaurant. She was so happy to see me and said, "I just want to thank you for what you did for my family." I must have done something, but I don't remember what it was. I do remember they were having a rough time of it.

About the same time that Carol came to work in the fibreglass business, Henry deBoon, Huibert's Brother, sold his pizza shop in Edmonton. He had part interest in the fibreglass business so he came to work there as well. So started the comparing of making pizzas and sauces. All the while we were fibreglassing.

After a year of going to Weight Watchers and losing all that weight accumulated in the pizza shop, I joined the Wetaskiwin Solo Club. I started going to dances because I needed to find some kind of outlet. Also the kids didn't need me as much now that they were growing up. And it seemed there were years of just work. Well, I did enjoy those dances and picnics the Solo Club had for single-parent families. I met a lot of nice people. One fellow from Red Deer came calling, but when he wanted to take me to meet his parents, I had to write a Dear John letter. Next time I saw him at one of those dances, he looked very crestfallen. I had one date with a man who invited me over for dinner at his place to introduce me to his six or eight kids. As soon as I walked in the door, he put an apron on me. *I* didn't put it on — *he* put it on me. I remember that. It was our first and last date. That's one apron string I didn't get tied to!

Meanwhile Henry and I were working and visiting together every day at the fibreglass shop.

In the winter of '74, I took a ceramics course, which I enjoyed. I also took a women's wood-working course. I made a corner shelf, a nut bowl and a bread board. I really enjoyed working with wood.

Chickens in the Living Room

One spring I decided to raise chickens. I ordered 100 baby chicks and, wouldn't you know, the weather turned cold and the brooder house at Ed Billsborrow's farm wasn't ready. So I put the chicks in our dining room! Well, that hit the local newspapers. I was a little embarrassed but what the

heck. I made a fence of cardboard and put newspapers on the floor. I think I had the chicks there for about two weeks. In the fall, Ron and Doris Marshall helped me kill and freeze them. I knew the Marshalls from work. They took a percentage of the chickens for helping me.

What an undertaking. I killed the chickens using a method I learned from Granny Long on the farm. I laid a broom handle over their necks, pressing down on it with both feet, and quickly jerked up on the chicken's feet. The body went one way, and the head went the other, with the eyes blinking in protest! I couldn't stand to cut their heads off, so I had to do it this way.

Well, we were never hungry, with a garden and meat in the deep freeze. I didn't have money to buy much fruit so I paid the kids five or 10 cents a cup to pick wild raspberries and I made some jam. I even picked rose hips and made jam out of them but the kids didn't think much of it. I tried to tell them rose hips have more vitamin C than oranges!

Ida's Growing Up

As for Ida, well I needed a shotgun to keep the boys away. One fellow that stands out in my memory was very outgoing even to the point of taking Ida's shoes off and kissing her feet. I think she got rid of him quick like.

I'm afraid Ida broke a few hearts in those days. One thing Ida did around this time was to host at the Olympic Games which was a real highlight in her life. I remember her being real excited about that.

Antics of Ellen and David

Nisku was a good place for boys and girls to express themselves. Ellen and David were both very active. I remember Ellen coming in once after she ripped her pants off on a barbed wire fence. Another time, she came in all scraped and bruised because she fell off the top of a train. She used to run along the tops of train boxcars like I did when I was a child. One time, out of pity, she collected up all the

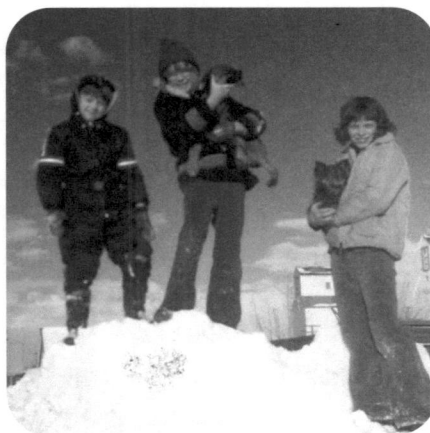

"He showered me with expensive gifts. Initially, I liked the attention, but his foot fetish did me in, so I broke up with him. But to this day, I still buy the same fragrance of perfume he gave me."

Ida

"I remember Mom as not being that lenient on me. For this, I am thankful. Looking back it was probably more than due."

David

"When I was 14, I got my first job washing dishes at the Airway Motor Inn. Later, I did chambermaiding and waitressing. I was very proud of myself and bought most of my own things with the money I made."

Ellen

Opposite page:
(top) Carol admiring my garden

(middle) Ida (age 16), grade 11, 1974

(bottom right) Ellen (age 12), grade 7, 1973

(bottom left) David (age 9), grade 3, 1974

This page:
(top) Here's our babies:. 100 chicks in the dining room, May 1973

(bottom) David and Ellen with neighbour Iris McConnell, 1972

gopher traps that were set out by the granary operator. I hated to make her do it, but she had to go give them back. The thing I always remember is the aptitude Ellen had to pick out a tune by ear. I remember Ellen and David squabbling a lot at Nisku. It almost drove me up the wall. She would call him "Snib" and he would call her "Ellen smellen, fat watermelon." She was far from fat!

David had a friend named Andrew Bonnett. They would put a nail on the end of a broom handle and go out in the fields and spear mice. Great fun, eh! Once, David built an underground fort. Why, the first time a big rain come, it flooded. Sometimes, there was trouble, like the time Craig, the boy next door, and David proceeded to throw stones and knock out $200 worth of streetlights in the Nisku industrial park. That hurt my pocketbook. David had been saving $25 to $30 in Mountie quarters. I made him give those up to help pay for the streetlights — painful, I guess, but a learning experience. I can't remember for sure, but I think I eventually gave the coins back to him.

Enter Henry

My relationship with Henry started very casually. It was not love at first sight. After awhile, the relationship grew and I realized I was in love with him. I didn't know how he felt until the Christmas of 1974, when he came to the door with a package behind his back, to be put under the tree. I thought, "Uh, oh! He's interested." But of course I was interested too. He gave me a watch. I was so thrilled. Before that, he wasn't able to show his feelings because he was scared to death of a woman with five kids, three at home. Also, he was married twice before. His last marriage failed and there were teenage kids in that too. But fate took a hand in our relationship and on February 14, 1975, we became engaged.

I phoned Linda in Trenton, Ontario, where she was posted with the military. She was working in an office and she yelled out to everyone, "Wow, my mother's finally making us legitimate." That was met with a lot of laughs, I am sure.

Letter to Linda, April 7, 1975

My Dearest Linda,

I know you must be dying for the days to pass. I am getting pretty excited myself. Tomorrow, Henry and I are going for our blood test and also to rent a wedding cake and buy a box spring and mattress. I am afraid I am running pretty tired these days. Getting married is kind of taxing on an old gal, you know. I just mailed some wedding invitations. David has a new suit. Boy, is he ever proud of it. Ida will be back on Friday. Sure miss her. Well Linda, soon you will be here too. Can't wait. So will see you soon.

Love Mom

Henry and I were undertaking some marriage counselling since we both had come out of failed relationships. I found the counselling good up to a point. Henry was Presbyterian and I was United. We decided to find a church close to Nisku, one we could both go to. Henry's parents used to go to the Heimtal Moravian Church, which was about 15 minutes away from Nisku. This church was out in the country surrounded by a farming community. The minister of that church, Reverend Curt Vitt, married us on April 25, 1975.

I was 46 and Henry was 46. Our birthdays were one week apart. In fact I was one week older than he was. I always liked to tease him that during that week he would have to respect his elders. He would always say "Ya, ya!"

Wedding Day

Our wedding was nice, and since money was still very tight I was always improvising. I went to a thrift shop and found a beautiful white wedding gown. I paid $25 for it. I didn't want to be married in white so I spent $15 and had the gown dyed blue and had a four-inch piece of lace added to the bottom because it was too short. Cathy made my headpiece. So for under $50, I had a lovely outfit for our wedding.

A wedding is never without some hitches. My car played out on the way to church and just barely made it. When we got there, Linda was probably nervous and played the music fairly fast. Someone said afterwards they felt like getting up and dancing. One of the songs she played was "Hymn to Joy." Pamela deBoon was the flower girl and David was the ring-bearer. Huibert stood up for Henry and Carol Tylke and Doris Marshal stood up for me. Our reception was at the Spruce Dale Hall, five miles west of Nisku.

One nice thing about the wedding was that

"As I was playing The Wedding March for Mom and Henry's wedding, the small mirror that was sitting on top of the piano came crashing down on my hands!"

Linda

Opposite page:
(top) David and Ellen squabbling, 1974

(middle) Henry and I on our engagement day, February 14, 1975

This page:
(top) The neighbour ladies held a wedding shower for me.

(middle right) wedding day, April 25, 1975

(bottom) Granny Long and Frankie; Henry and I with David as ring-bearer

"It took awhile to get used to Henry but, boy, did he ever grow on me over time. He cried easily when something moved him, which endeared me to him, and he had a generous heart. But then there was his habit of licking his teeth at the table. At 14, I was just plain grossed out!"

Ellen

"Henry had a great sense of humour. I sensed that he was someone Mom could trust."

Cathy

"Henry was a good-hearted man. He didn't express his feelings too well but then again I'm not sure he was asked too often. To me, Henry was someone who spent more effort listening than speaking. I think Henry had a great deal of wisdom to offer our family."

David

Granny Long, Bob's mother, was in attendance. I hadn't invited her because I didn't think she would want to come. But I was very pleased when she asked if she could come. Over the years, I felt her support. She didn't seem to blame me for leaving Bob although she was sad about it. This meant a lot to me.

Henry and I went to BC for our honeymoon. I had never been to BC in the spring. I was awestruck, as all the apple trees and cherry trees were in bloom. I had never seen that before. We stayed in Vancouver and Henry took me to a boat that had been converted into a restaurant. I remember sampling many different kinds of seafood.

Adjustments

Henry was a hard-working Dutch fellow. He laid down only two expectations before we were married, which were that the coffee pot always be on and that he got a steak fried for dinner every night. I figured we couldn't afford steak for the whole family so most of the time we ate hamburger while Henry had steak. Of course there were some adjustments for us but out of our love and respect for each other we worked them through. It was such a wonderful thing to have a good responsible man to share my load. But there were some trying times. At the end of one of our first meals, Henry flipped out his false teeth and proceeded to lick them off, much to the dismay of the kids. I got Henry in a corner and asked him to please clean his teeth in the bathroom. He had been living alone for two years and I guess you have some habits that are not in good taste.

It was so nice having a man around the house and nicer to have someone to share the responsibilities with. Henry was not a threat to my security. Also he let me raise the kids and very rarely intervened. Only once did I see him lose his temper, when David was talking in a disrespectful way. I guess it scared David and also Ida, Ellen and myself.

Henry Renovates the House

When Henry moved in, he was scared of the wiring in the house so he had an electrician come in and change it. Some feat in a 10-room house. It cost $8000! Henry was very happy renovating the place. It was built in 1928 and was French provincial-style. Each window had four bars at the top and one pane below. Henry changed the windows in the kitchen, living room and dining room into picture windows. Four new windows — what a transformation. Then he built a patio door off the dining room and eventually built a fibreglass deck. Later, he added a new back porch and had the house insulated. We also got a new rug in the living and dining room area. Oh, and I shouldn't forget, he put in a bathtub. Before that, we only had a shower. Much later, he built a garage and a fibreglass greenhouse in the shape of a pyramid. Boy, what a worker. He must have put $30,000 in that house. He loved to work, then come in, have a bath, and watch hockey.

The deBoon Family Welcomes Us

Henry was from a large family that was quite close. They welcomed us with open arms. It gave me a real sense of family. At that point in my life, I really appreciated this. I really liked everybody but I got to know Bertha and Huibert best because they lived so close by. I have always thought they were the salt of the earth.

Henry's dad raised all kinds of birds and he got me interested in raising cockatiels. First he gave me one that he called Hank. Well, Hank turned out to be Henrietta! Then Henry gave me a male cockatiel and that began my experience of raising birds. Henry's dad sold young cockatiels to pet stores and he took my young birds also. Henry and I turned the downstairs room into a bird room. Henry made big wooden cages and, every Saturday morning, I had to clean these cages and the whole room too. What a mess. And also, cockatiels are very noisy! But we had a lot of fun with those birds.

Later, I gave up all but two of my birds. I kept one grey and one yellow one who were brothers. The grey one could sing the first line of "Obla Di, Obla Dah" and both birds could say, "Hello pretty boy" and "Dumb birdie." One of them used to mimic the sound and action of me grating carrots! One time, I went on holidays and left the birds with a friend. When I returned and walked in the house, both birds flew against the side of the cage and excitedly repeated the phrase, "Hello pretty boy." I realized at that point that they recognized me.

The Heimtal Moravian Church

Through the years that we were at the Heimtal Moravian church, I taught Sunday school and was a Sunday school superintendent for five years along with two others. When it came time for Christmas and Easter programs we worked together. Other than that, we took turns doing things. Henry was an elder for a period of time

"Two weeks after Henry and Mary were married, I stopped to visit them at their home with an acquaintance that didn't know them. After we left, I said to him that Henry and Mary had just been married for two weeks. He looked at me with amazement and said he thought they had been married all their lives. That was the way we felt about Mary and her family; it felt like they belonged as part of our family right from the start. Years after our brother died, Mary and her children remain a very loved and important part of our family."

Huibert deBoon, Henry's brother

"I have very fond memories of Camp Van Es. There was always plenty of pranks, singing, games and group activities and that made it a very memorable part of my childhood."

David

Opposite page:

(top) Me and 2 of our cockatiels

(bottom left) David (age 10), grade 4, 1975

(bottom right) David (age 11), grade 5, 1976

"My English wasn't too good, of course. I asked cab drivers and they didn't speak hardly any good English either. I was in the mood to go back to Holland! Finally, one cab driver knew, and he took to Nisku and dropped me off on a muddy road at the end of the street. Then, a dirty little boy came up to me and said, "Are you Richard?"

Richard, Mary's stepson who lives in Holland.

"I remember asking, "Why do all the cars have kisses?" I meant why were so many cars dented. Everyone laughed, of course. The bread in Canada was not that good. But I remember putting it with pepperoni and cheese in the microwave. Then it was ok."

Richard

"Imagine me at 15 years old, with my understated Canadian sensibilities, clashing with Richard who was 17 years old, with his direct Dutch sensibilities. And each of us stubborn as an ox. I won sometimes and Richard won sometimes. Within the next few years, I plan to visit Richard in Holland, where I expect we'll argue over where to go and what to eat— I look forward to this!"

Ellen

and he taught an adult class. David was confirmed in this church. One of the songs they played at his confirmation was "The Family of God." Every summer we were able to send David to Camp Van Es, east of Edmonton. The girls were getting too old for the change, I guess. They had chosen their own paths.

Richard Comes to Stay

In early July of '75, Henry's 17-year-old son, Richard, arrived from Holland. We weren't expecting him till the next day. So naturally we weren't at the airport to meet him so he got a cab. When he was walking along Nisku Road, he saw a little kid all covered in dirt. It was David. Then he came into the backyard where Henry and I were in the garden transplanting tomatoes. I had mud clear up to my knees and my hands were all muddy. Well, here was this tall, long-haired boy standing on the back step. All I could do was hug him, dirt and all. We must have made quite a first impression!

Richard was a nice fellow, but he was going through a lot of teenaged changes in his life and he had a lot of different expectations than I was used to. I think there was a cultural clash. For one of our first meals together, I made baked potatoes and corn on the cob. This came as a big shock to Richard, who was used to corn and potato skins being fed to pigs. I have to admit he tried my patience to the nth degree. Naturally, because I had teenagers at home, there were some conflicts with a new teenager in the house.

That same summer, Huibert and Henry put a two-storey houseboat on the Saskatchewan River in Edmonton to be part of Klondike Days river-raft races. David and Henry dressed in Klondike clothes and I had an orange square-dance dress on with a big hat. Well, Richard decided to go for a swim. He laid his blue jeans on the top deck and dove in. When he got out, just before putting his pants on, Huibert started going very fast and Richard's pants flew into the river. You know, we never did find them. Richard had to put a coat around his bottom and we went over to Ida's apartment in Edmonton and he borrowed a pair of her jeans. They were halfway up his legs! We called them his flood pants. After this we all went to the Sunday Promenade. We teased Richard that he had to come to Canada to lose his pants.

We took Richard through the mountains and into BC. In one restaurant we went to he said, "I am going to have me a real steke" (he couldn't pronounce steak). I must

"Losing my pants was terrible. That was really embarrassing. The elastic on my underwear wasn't very good. I almost stretched my t-shirt till it came off!"

Richard

"Everything was so big. The roads, the cars, everything. I couldn't believe my eyes. So different than in Holland."

Conny, Mary's daughter-in-law

have fed him too much hamburger before that. So he ordered Salisbury steak, and when it come, he yelled out loud, "hamburger." Everyone in the restaurant stopped eating and looked at us. Maybe I shouldn't have laughed but I couldn't help myself.

During this time, I decided to start taking Dutch lessons. I had to stop because Henry was having some problems with his digestion and had to have an operation.

Richard had a girlfriend, Conny, and at the time she was in Africa with her parents. I think he was very lonesome for her. After 11 months he went back home to Holland. He eventually married Conny and they have two children, Brenda and Wendy. There is a nice picture of them in chapter seven. Richard has grown up to be a very hard worker and a responsible husband and father. Before they had the kids, Richard and Conny came to Canada for a holiday, which was really nice.

Opposite page:
(top) David (age 12), confirmation day, 1977

(bottom) Ellen (age 15), grade 9, 1976

This page:
(all photos) Klondike Days in Edmonton, 1976

This page:
(top) This was taken around the time David went to get Ria-Mae in 1979.

(middle left) Four generations: Granny Long, me, Cathy and Ria-Mae, 1980.

(middle right) Bob took this photo of Ellen, Ida, Linda and Cathy in Claresholm on the day of Granny Long's funeral, 1985.

(bottom) Darren (age 9 or 10)

Cathy

In the late seventies, Cathy was living in Sooke, BC, which is north of Victoria. On May 9, 1979 she had a baby girl, Ria-Mae. Henry and I drove out to the Island when Ria was 10 days old. Cathy seemed very un-happy so I asked her if she would like to come back to Alberta and stay with us for a while until she was able to get established on her own. We took Cathy and the baby to a parade. There were 60 bands in that parade — they really went all out in that city for the Victoria Day celebration. We drove around to a lot of places on that trip. It was blackberry season and I was out every morning before breakfast so we had blackberries with our cereal. Henry was disgusted with blackberry picking. Of course we didn't have the right clothes for the job so the scratches we got were something else.

We also went deep-sea fishing on that trip. Now, that was a new and interesting experience. The captain yelled, "Quick, here comes Jaws," and then flipped a three-foot baby shark in the boat. That scared us all pretty good before the captain flipped it back into the water. And now the truth comes out: Henry and I never caught a darn thing on that trip. Oh well, it was fun anyway. We picked a lot of fruit on the trip. Meantime, Ida and Ellen were at home picking and freezing all my beans and peas. They were fed up to the teeth with them I guess.

Six months later, David and Paul (Bob's step-son from his second marriage) flew out and brought Ria back by plane. I understand it was quite an experience for two teenage boys who were only around 14 at the time. Especially since Cathy forgot to send diapers! During a stop over in Calgary, somebody saw the dilemma and offered a diaper.

Cathy, in the meantime, came through the mountains in a very loaded-down car. I believe she had car trouble too and had to leave half her stuff someplace. I will never forget when she arrived in front of the house with the car about six inches off the pavement. Was she ever loaded down! Cathy and Ria lived with us for a time. That was when I discovered how much Henry loved babies. With all the grandchildren he knew, he would hold them a lot and play with them. He could really get them laughing. Often times, he could get a baby to stop crying.

After three months, Cathy got an apartment in Leduc. There she met a fellow called Jim Rice. She had a baby boy by him named Mathew, born on September 23, 1981. He was a lovely baby, much loved by all. Cathy and Jim broke up at the time of Mathew's birth.

Jim had a boy named Darren who came over from Ireland when he was nine to stay with his dad and Cathy. I remember that he was a very bright boy. He liked hockey. Darren and I built a bird house together that I put out in Bashaw many years later. After Jim and Cathy broke up, Jim and Darren lived on their own. It was a bad situation and social services gave Darren to me to look after for a short time before he was sent back to his mom in Ireland. Over the years, I kept in touch with Darren through Christmas cards and the occasional letter. He joined the English Army. We seem to have lost touch now.

When Mathew and Ria-Mae were seven and nine, Cathy married Bernie Kowalewski and they live in the house in Nisku. They met while working together in a commercial sign painting company. Cathy got a certificate from the Northern Alberta Institute of Technology (NAIT) in commercial sign painting and had her own business in that for a while. Now, she works for the Better Business Bureau. One of the ways that Cathy's artistic aptitude shows itself is in her love of flowers, fashionable clothes and anything beautiful. Bernie is a wonderful person who loves the kids. He does photography and is a great gardener. Cathy and Bernie play in a blues band. Cathy is very self-sufficient and responsible. In 1998, Ria-Mae married Scott Cranston and they live in Edmonton.

"My very strong feeling around her is one of peace. I feel that she's a peacemaker and peacekeeper by nature. Being around her is restful. She's like a quiet, safe island in a stormy sea. She's the quintessential mother. You always feel like she's going to make things better. She's like a mother to me."

Bernie, Mary's son-in-law

"She's sweeter than jam!"

Granddaughter Ria-Mae, 20

"When I stayed over, I'd always hear her singing and talking to her birds down in the basement."

Grandson Mathew, 17

This page:
(top left) Darren (age 18)

(middle) Cathy, Ria-Mae and Mathew, 1983

(above) Cathy graduated from NAIT in 1986

(bottom left) Cathy and Bernie's wedding, with Ria-Mae (9) as flower girl and Mathew (7) as ring-bearer, 1988

"When we were in the pizza shop, I remember Mom telling me, "the customer is always right" and thinking that was a stupid piece of wisdom. However, it sure does help me in my business today."

Linda

"Thinking back, I'd have to say Mom turned every low blow of life into a bouquet of love."

Linda

"Tenacity in the face of adversity—she's a living example of the Golden Rule: Do unto others . . ."

Peter, Mary's son-in-law

"I enjoy playing cards with her. She's nice and she's lively."

Grandson Keegan, 14

"She's very loving and caring and she's very funny. She loves to joke."

Grandson Peter Jr., 15

"Fruit ambrosia!!!!

Grandson John, 19, when asked about what stands out for him about his Granny.

This page:

(top) Linda joined the military in the early 1970s

(bottom left) Linda (age 21) got her wings in 1975

(bottom right) Linda and Peter

Linda

When Linda first joined the military, she was stationed in Cornwallis, Nova Scotia. One time I sent her some home-baked goods through the mail. There was a mail strike, and by the time she got the package, everything was moldy. Later, she was stationed in Ontario. One of the jobs Linda had in the military was as a flight attendant. She travelled all over the world. One of her trips was to Brazil with the Minister of External Affairs. Linda was very generous-hearted and brought me beautiful gifts from all over the world.

It was in Ontario that Linda met her future husband, Peter Portlock . They flew to Alberta to be married. After they were married, I flew out to Ottawa to be with Peter and Linda for a week. They couldn't get any time off while I was there so I hopped buses and found my way all over Ottawa. I took a tour of the Parliament Buildings one day and the next day I got a free pass from the MP of my home district to attend Parliament in session. It was really interesting watching the opposition try to bring in a vote of non-confidence against Trudeau. When I was leaving I saw Ed Broadbent, the NDP leader, in the hallway. I shook hands and spoke briefly with him.

Linda and Peter took me to an Austrian restaurant one night, where someone was playing old Austrian songs on the accordion. It was sure nice. People were clapping to

the music, singing and eating all at once. I found in the short time I was there that people I met were really helpful and friendly. Ottawa is a very beautiful city. Many of the churches are built of stone or brick. There are a lot of red brick houses. Huge ones too. No wonder they need a lot of oil down there to heat their houses.

Peter and Linda now live in Edmonton with their three sons, John, Peter Jr. and Keegan. Linda practices law and has tremendous compassion for helping others, especially people from different cultures. She is a very responsible person. Linda and Peter are both very musical. Peter has enriched our family in many ways. He is the director of the Labour Arbitration Board of Alberta. He is also the organist and choir director for Grace United Church.

Ida

When Ida moved out of home, she lived in Edmonton with a friend named Vivi and worked at the Royal Bank. Ida and Vivi took a trip to Denmark together. That was a highlight. Ida went down to live with Linda in Trenton, Ontario for a year. She worked in a bank there too. While she was there, Henry and I made a surprise visit for Thanksgiving. I baked pies and packed up some garden vegetables. When we went through the airport security, why, this cabbage and other vegetables and the pies showed up on the monitor for all to see. I didn't know that was going to happen! On that trip, we visited Niagara Falls, which was a thrilling thing to do. It was fall time and I couldn't get over the red colour of the maple leaves and the big wagons loaded high with bright orange pumpkins that we saw.

A short time after that, Ida went to NAIT and studied accounting. She did real well at that because she's very good with numbers. Later, Ida moved to Claresholm

" Around the time I was starting NAIT, I was going through an internal crisis. I realized that there was nothing on this earth that could make me happy. Mom recognized this as God's call for my life ... and she was very right."

Ida

This page:

(top left) Linda and Peter's wedding, 1976

(top right) John, Peter Jr., Peter Sr., Linda and Keegan, 1998

(middle right) Linda and Peter, university graduation, 1985

(bottom left) Ida was the treasurer of the NAIT Student Association, 1981.

(bottom right) Ida graduated from NAIT in 1981.

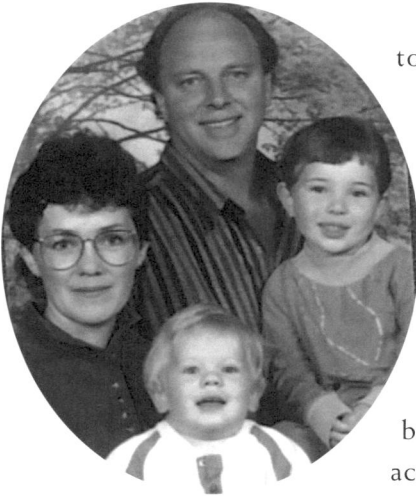

"Mom has always had an incredible capacity to love unconditionally."

Ida

"She likes to sing a lot. She's always funny and telling jokes. She's good at knitting — she's teaching me how to do it."

Granddaughter Megan, nine

"I liked when she would draw pictures for me."

Grandson Jordan, seven

"This is my impression of Mom: I see her zipping down the highway of life, with no worries of the stop signs slowing her down. Ah! The adventure continues . . . Let us know what's over the next hill and around the next corner, Mom."

Rob, Mary's son-in-law

to look after Granny Long. There, she met and married Rob Howe and they have two children, Megan and Jordan. In my mind, Rob is a very solid person and a good father and provider. Rob and Ida run a carpentry contracting business in Leduc. Rob's accomplishments in the carpentry field can be seen all over the town of Leduc and the Nisku Industrial Park. One thing that stands out for me about Ida is that she has turned into an excellent cook. This is funny because she was turned off at the very thought of cooking in her younger years. So far, of all my kids, Ida's the one who likes gardening the best. Ida has developed into a wonderful, responsible person.

David's Trip to Ottawa

David flew to Ottawa in the summer of 1979 for 10 days to stay with Linda and her husband Peter. David's seat

In September of '85, Ida sent me a very special poem written by Susan Schultz. I will write it here, as it touched me so.

To My Mother

For as long as I can remember
You were always by my side
To give me support
to give me confidence
To give me help
For as long as I can remember
Your were always the person I looked up to
So strong, so sensitive, so pretty
For as long as I can remember
And still today
You are everything a mother should be
For as long as I can remember
You always provided stability within our family
Full of laughter
Full of tears
Full of love
Whatever I have become is because of you
And I thank you forever for our relationship.

partner on the plane was Gordon Taylor (former minister of highways and MP for the Bow River constituency around Calgary). When they got to Ottawa, Gordon Taylor took David and Linda on a personal tour of the Parliament Buildings. David got to sit in Joe Clark's chair even before Joe Clark did. He saw places that even the general tourists don't get to go. After that Mr. Taylor took David and Linda to lunch and of course David embarrassed Linda by eating everything in sight. Oh well, growing boys! Mr. Diefenbaker died while David was in Ottawa and

Peter was involved in the funeral in some way. All in all, the airplane flights and the many sights were a broadening experience for a boy of David's age.

Problems Next Door

When David was a teenager, one major concern to me was his adventure of getting high on sniffing gasoline with his friend Darrin Kasprick and some others. I was very much upset, as this can kill you or make a vegetable out of your brains. David spent a lot of time at Darrin's — no mother there, and a father that worked. I think there was probably shenanigans going on but I couldn't barge in another's house. But maybe I should have. Darrin used to call me "Mom," and one Mother's Day, he gave me a swan planter for my deck.

Later, when David and Darrin were around 16, Darrin was in a car accident. He was driving with three passengers and they ran into the side of a train. Darrin was killed instantly. I assume because of very loud music, they didn't hear the train, or maybe they were racing to beat it. Of course David was devastated. I felt so bad for him. The funeral was in Leduc and we had the lunch at our house after.

The Luc Family From Vietnam

Shortly after I got home from Ottawa, I joined an organization in Leduc called People Helping People. We brought a family of Vietnamese boat people over from a refugee camp in Hong Kong and helped them get established. They were called boat people because they escaped the war in Vietnam by crossing the ocean in boats. The family that we helped had a mom and dad, seven kids and an 82-year-old grandmother. What an emotional experience. They told of being on the ocean for 35 days with 32 other people in a small boat. Many people were very seasick and the family almost lost their baby boy. As they approached the shores of Hong Kong, the boat hit a rock and broke in two. But everyone was saved! They lived in a refugee camp for nine months before coming to Canada. I helped drive the family from the airport into Leduc. Years later, the dad told me that when he saw the wheat fields, he was afraid that he and his family were going to be sent out to the fields to work.

The mother and the dad worked for us in the fibreglass plant. The mother couldn't stand the smell and didn't stay very long. Later I think she worked at the Leduc Inn. I gave the father the Canadian name of Luke which was close to his last name of Luc. As we worked together, I taught Luke to speak English. He also tried to teach me Vietnamese. Well, that was a hoot. I got invited over many Saturdays and the family tried to teach me to eat with chopsticks. I was useless. They even got me to try the baby's chopsticks. Well, I could still hardly eat. Of course, I laughed at myself and they laughed their heads off at me. Years later, I went into a restaurant in Leduc and found the Luc family running the place. They insisted on buying my supper. It was a nice reunion.

"What a privilege it was to see the House of Commons and witness John Diefenbaker's state funeral and go roller-skating with Peter and Linda who gave it their best effort for my sake. Oh, the '70s."

David

"It rocked my world when Darrin was killed. At that age of 16, I didn't know how to deal with his loss. What a terrible thing for his family to deal with as well."

David

Opposite page:
(top) Ida, Rob, Megan and Jordan, 1994

(middle) Ida and Rob's wedding, with Granny Long, 1981

(bottom) David (age 13 or 14), grade 7

This page:
Darrin Kasprick used to call me "Mom."

Our First Caribbean Cruise

Henry and I decided to go on a cruise in 1980. The travel agent told us Canadians really liked this particular ship, the Veracruz. Well, we went for it. If we only had known, we were had! Still, what an experience for a person who only knew camping trips as a holiday, to then go on a big boat so far from home. Of course we went on an economy package and we sure found out you get only what you pay for. The ship was small and our room was in the lower floor by the engine room. The first night our mattress threw us together in the middle. We had to call for a piece of plywood. Our bed filled the room with only about a 12-inch space around the bed. The bathroom was so small you could go to the bathroom, have a shower and brush your teeth all at once. And the engine roared all night. Ugh!

The two-week trip wasn't bad otherwise. We got acquainted with one of the waiters on the ship named Martin. It was his first time serving meals on a ship. I remember one evening I wore a pearl necklace and, mind you, they were not real pearls. You should have seen his eyes pop open and his mouth drop. At the end of our trip he dove in the ocean and brought me two bags of lovely shells. When we got home we were very brown and glad to be home. I kept in touch with Martin by letters for a while.

Our Second Caribbean Cruise

Our second cruise came a year later in the middle of February. This time we went first class on the Princess Line, a boat that was a sister to the Love Boat. There was no comparison from the first trip. On this trip we went through the Panama Canal, to Acapulco, up to Los Angeles, and home by airplane.

I remember on one of the islands we stepped into a taxi cab and there on the seat was a packet of travellers' cheques valued at $500. We quickly hid them from the eyes of the cab driver because we weren't sure if we could trust him. When we got back to our ship we took the cheques to the captain but the name was not on the passenger list. Lucky enough, the Love Boat was

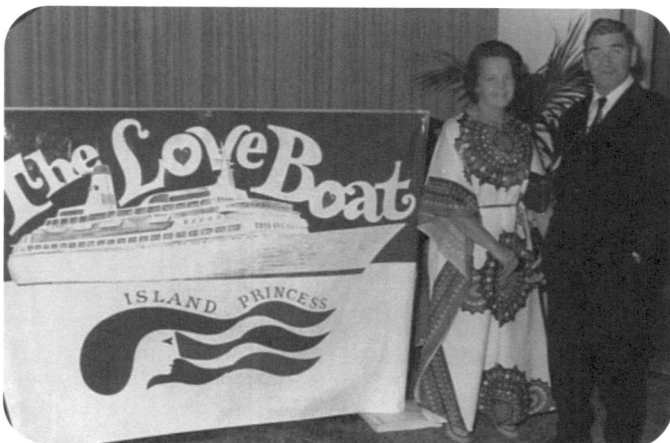

anchored behind us and Henry went over there and sure enough the owner of the cheques was there. A few weeks later we received a lovely letter from a fellow from Nebraska thanking us and saying that his whole holiday would have been spoiled but for our honesty.

One day they asked all Canadian passengers to gather in one of the lounges. They separated us by provinces and asked us to circulate. I stood in front of this couple and the woman said, "I know you! You're Mary Middleton. We were in the first grade in the little brick schoolhouse in Carmangay." Well, we talked for over an hour swapping stories about mud pies and skipping ropes. What a delightful experience this was.

On this trip, I took a two-hour course in scuba diving, took my courage in hand, said a prayer and ventured 30 feet to the ocean floor. They gave me dog food as bait and hundreds and hundreds of the most beautiful coloured fish descended on me. I should say, before going any further, I had to have 10 pounds of extra weight put on my waist in order to make me go down. I have to tell you the sensation I got while on the ocean floor. It felt like I was in a cathedral with the rays of sunshine diffusing through the water. There were many beautiful coral reefs and so many wonderful kinds of fish. I also saw a black spiny urchin rolling over the sand. And here I was, 52 years of age, and yet able to experience this. Wow!

This trip took us to many Caribbean islands plus stopped at the top of South America where we went into the city of Caracas. It was 45 miles to the city from where we docked and on either side of the road there were 10-foot by 10-foot brick huts attached one to the next. The plains people came there to live hoping for work and ended up living in slum-like conditions. When we got to the city there were marble streets and many statues of various leaders. Many apartments had boxes and boxes of flowers growing. Very colourful.

We were near the equator and it was extremely hot. Henry sat in the shade for awhile and still ended up with severe sunburn. You should have seen his legs and arms. They turned purple and he got very ill. I had to get a doctor. Violent chills came on him and he spent three days in bed before he felt normal. Then he couldn't go out in the sun anymore.

After going through the Panama Canal, we travelled to Acapulco and there watched the cliff divers and children at the side of the road. We were warned not to give them anything because back in the hills they came from beautiful wealthy homes. How true this is, I really don't know. Next we were at a place called the Baja Peninsula. We experienced a terrible wind, which

Opposite page:
(top) Henry and I with Martin from St. Lucia

(middle) The Princess Line

(bottom) On the Princess Line

This page:
(top) Henry and I scuba diving!

(bottom) On the Princess Line

"I'll never forget the sense of fear and urgency I felt the day we drove Henry to the hospital. We just held his hands and talked calmly to him. The trip took 10 minutes — it felt like 10 hours."

Ellen

made most of the people seasick. Henry and I didn't get sick. I have a tape recording of that wind as I stepped outside long enough to tape this storm. Finally we docked, or should I say we weighed anchor, and smaller boats took us to shore where the local people took us in smaller boats to see the seals and pelicans on the rocks. It was a beautiful sight. The next stop was Los Angeles where we spent three hours in Disneyland then flew home to Edmonton. We were met by the kids. I guess I had a colourful straw hat on and a very dark tan; I got some comments on that. I was sure glad to see my family. There really is no place like home.

Henry's Health Falters

One day, in January of 1982, Henry was outside working on the sewer system. It was very cold, 20° below (Fahrenheit), and there was a cold wind. Henry smoked and he was always coughing a lot. He came in and sat down to dinner. He couldn't eat and said, "I don't feel so well," and went into the living room. His colour was grey. I said "Have you got pneumonia?"

"No," he said, "I wonder if it's my heart." Well, did I ever move!

Core, Henry's younger brother was working at the shop. I phoned him and he came over. Core was not much help because he had an anxiety attack so I had to drive the car. I didn't have time to warm the car up so I scraped a small space in the window and I drove 100 miles an hour to Leduc. They gave Henry a shot, called an ambulance, and we were on the way to Edmonton University Hospital. After we got there Henry had a massive heart attack and was clinically dead for one-and-a-half minutes. They brought him back with the shock paddles on his chest. He finally came around and got some better. But Henry's lifestyle had to change. No more steaks or a pack of cigarettes a day.

The coming summer we went on a short holiday to the mountains. When we got home, we found out there was a big rainstorm and the sump pump in the basement was broke down. Henry got into high gear and pulled the sump pump from the sewer. Well, this exertion brought on another heart attack. Ellen, Les Csole, and I drove Henry to the Leduc hospital. History repeated itself with another rush trip to Edmonton by ambulance. The specialist took me aside and said, "As sick as Henry is, I can only give him a 50-50 chance of survival but I must operate immediately." So Henry had triple bypass. After the operation they let me in the intensive care room. He was so full of tubes. I held his hand and sang songs to him. What a very tough time for both of us.

The next few weeks Henry was in and out of intensive care. Finally after six weeks he came home. He was pretty weak. He had a shower one Saturday night and when he came out in the kitchen he passed out on the floor. After that I sponge-bathed him until he got stronger. He was even too weak at first to lift the coffee pot to pour a cup of coffee. At this time, I was almost too nervous to even go out and get groceries. Then he got an infection in his leg. You see, when he had the triple bypass, they took a vein from the left leg to repair his heart. Well, I did a lot of praying at this time. Henry felt too weak to go to a doctor so I had to take my courage in hand and treat this myself. I put hot salt packs on this infection several times a day and finally it got better.

Henry was a year at home before going back to work. He worked on jigsaw puzzles and watched the soaps. In the meantime, I was still working at Versatile Fibreglass.

My Ankle Plays Out

I guess from being on my feet on cement floors, my one ankle played out. In the late summer of 1983, the specialist found out the bone in my leg at the ankle joint was busted through. On October 31, 1983, I was operated on. My ankle was separated and they found a hole the size of a loonie in it. The doctor cleaned the bone chips out and I was told not to walk on it for three months so the bone and bone marrow would heal itself. So began a learning experience on crutches.

Life is harsh sometimes, but with perseverance and faith that there is a brighter tomorrow, we can pull through. And of course everything has a funny side. When I first came home I went to the washroom and was trying to manipulate my trousers standing on one leg. I leaned on the top of the clothes hamper that was in front of me. Well, the hinge was broken and I fell headlong into the hamper! The next challenge was getting upstairs to bed. I sat down and bum-walked myself upstairs. That was okay, but then how to get myself up off the floor? I recall lying there laughing my fool head off. I can't remember what kid opened up a door and said, "What's the matter?" I crawled using one knee and dragging the other till I reached the bed. I dragged myself up on the bed with my arm and one leg. I did this for nearly three months.

During this time Ellen took me out on a toboggan all around Nisku — what a hoot! I wonder if she ever knew how great it was to get out of the house. Another time Ida took me to the West Edmonton Mall and pushed me in a wheelchair. She sure gave me quite a ride — many people gave us a wide berth.

Because of my ankle operation, I could no longer stand fibreglassing. I was 52 years old and I went to an evening class in the Leduc high school and got my typing 10. Then I started working in the office of Versatile Fibreglass. I liked it.

Thinking About Moving

During the economic turndown of the eighties, many oil wells shut down or pulled out for the States. A decision was made to close the Nisku branch of Versatile Fibreglass and put everything under one umbrella in Meeting Creek, Alberta. This meant that Henry and I had to think about moving.

Opposite page:
Ellen (age 18), grade 12, 1979

This page:
Ellen pulling me around Nisku after my ankle operation

"She's such a joyful, heart-warming person. You feel like you know her right away."

Julie Robinson, a friend of Ellen's who met Mary on one of her trips to Toronto.

"The older I get, the more I become like Mom. This pleases me."

Ellen

Opposite page:
(top left) Ellen and her partner, Eve

(top right) I loved riding all over Toronto on an electric cart. The car is Ellen's 1974 Dodge Dart which she drove until 1998

(middle right) Summer 1998

(bottom left) Ellen and Eve with Peter Jr. and Keegan, 1999

(bottom right) I surprised Ellen by turning up unexpectedly at a Toronto restaurant.

This page:
(top) I knit each of my kids an afghan.

(right) Ellen's university graduation, 1986

In August of 1983 we were on our way to BC for a holiday and we decided to drive through Bashaw to look for houses. Ida was riding with us as far as Calgary. We looked all through the town but didn't see anything. When we were driving out on Highway 21 Henry said, "I think I see a for sale sign that's fallen down in the grass at that place. Shall we go back and have a look?" We had a look and I immediately fell in love with that house. But they wanted $97,000 for it and that was too much for us. Well, we went on our holiday to Victoria. Linda and Peter were out there visiting Peter's folks. While we were all together, Linda said, "Mom, you are in love with that house — you better buy it."

We said, "Oh no, it's too much money."

When we got back Henry said maybe we should go down to Bashaw and take another look. So we did and there started the wheeling and dealing except there wasn't much wheeling. We put in a real low bid of $78,000, and they went for it. We made a deal that they could live free until the following spring or until they found another house. Then I started my dreaming about that beautiful house. In the winter, while recuperating from my ankle operation, I knit an afghan for each of my children and a rose, grey and white one for the house in Bashaw. In June of 1984, I asked Cathy if she would like to rent the Nisku house and that was a happy arrangement for her and the children.

On June 26, 1984, we moved to Bashaw. Everyone was worried how Henry would withstand this move, and guess what? I caved in, not him! I was the one who broke down and landed in the hospital for one week suffering from nervous exhaustion. Meanwhile Henry unpacked the boxes and settled the house pretty good.

When I moved from Nisku to Bashaw, I retired from the business world. The move to Bashaw was my 16th since I left my parents' home in Carmangay.

Ellen

At the time of the move, Ellen was still living at home and going to university in Edmonton, majoring in sociology. When she found out we had to move, she made arrangements to go live in Edmonton with Linda and Peter. Eventually, she won a

$10,000 scholarship to go to York University in Toronto. She moved there and never came back to live. I lost my baby girl! But she has come home often over the years and other family members and I have visited her in Toronto. It was amazing to see Ellen do so well at university because she had a lot of trouble in school as a child. I guess this was because things were so unsettled in our lives.

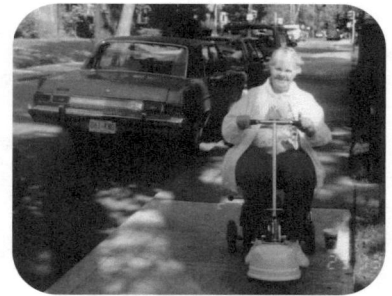

"She is a person with a great sense of fun and a wonderful spirit. The first time I met Mary was when she made a surprise trip to Toronto. I'll never forget being in a restaurant with Ellen, and of seeing Mary pop her head out from behind a pillar and start tip-toeing over to our table. Ellen just about fell off her chair! Once we were settled, Mary pulled a homemade pie out of her purse that she had brought all the way from Alberta. This was my introduction to Ellen's mom. Imagine my delight!"

Eve

On one of my trips to visit Ellen in Toronto, she rented a battery-operated cart. I had a blast on that thing! Ellen was teaching English as a second language at the time and couldn't get time off work. I went to class with her one day and she and the students showed me how to use the computer. That was my first and last time on a computer! Ellen's students gave me a gift of some towels and oven mitts.

Every day, I would go to the mall and buy a few groceries and make us supper. Some days I went swimming at the YMCA. The first day I went, I told them it was awfully expensive what they were charging. When I told them I was visiting from Alberta, they let me in free for the whole week! When Ellen came home, she would carry those heavy batteries up the stairs so they could be put on chargers. When she had time off, she would take apart the cart, load it into the car, and we would go different places like Ontario Place or the Island.

I found the people in Toronto very friendly, especially when I was riding the electric cart. They run and opened doors and made way for me in stores. Speaking of stores, in one place, the back wheel of the cart got caught on a clothing rack that was on wheels. Next thing I know, I'm dragging this rack clear across the room. I quickly got off the cart, unhitched the rack, and got out of the store. I didn't know the right place to put the rack so I just unhitched it and took off — I didn't want to get caught with the goods. Ha!

Now, Ellen works as the director of research for ABC CANADA, a national literacy foundation. She is about to have a book about education published. Ellen shows a lot of compassion for the needs of others. She is a caring person who has grown up to be a very responsible adult. She lives in Toronto with her partner, Eve Goldberg, who is a professional folk musician and office manager of a recording company. Eve is a nice person who is very musical and laughs very easily. Ellen and Eve are starting a new community chorus called Common Thread, which will have about 75 members. It's a group that will have youth and elderly people together, and everyone in between. It stands out in my mind that Ellen sometimes plays her accordion on the street to collect money for children's music programs.

Riding the Pails, I Mean Rails

The year I was in Toronto was the 125th anniversary of Canada's Confederation, so I decided to do something special and ride the train back to Alberta. The train travelled along nicely, until we stopped suddenly. We sat for hours with no one telling us why. Finally a big diesel engine came and towed us backwards for 400 miles to another track. We found out that there was a bridge washed out.

Finally, we were moving along again and it came time to turn in. Now, if you have never slept in one of those little rooms, you're in for an education, as indeed I was. The bed pulls down from the wall and covers the toilet. Click, and everything is in place. That was fine, until the middle of the night and the urge to go couldn't be put off. I got up and, wouldn't you know, I couldn't figure out how to make the bed go up. I buzzed the steward but that didn't work either. Heavens, what will I do? The public bathroom was at the other end of the car and I didn't have a housecoat. I grabbed the plastic garbage pail and set it on the middle of the bed. In your wildest imagination, you could never envision this rather heavy-set woman trying to ride this pail in a train lurching down the railway tracks in the middle of the night. Amazingly, I never even spilled a drop!

In the morning, I was talking to a woman in the lounge who said, "I was having such a time brushing my teeth because there was a wooden cover over the sink that only had holes where the taps would drip through." She didn't know enough to lift the cover off! I thought, her problem was nothing compared to mine but I was too embarrassed at the time to tell her anything. Now here I am telling it all.

Toshiaki Uchibi

This woman and I went to the dining car and sat with a couple and a Japanese boy who was about 20 or so. The couple asked if I knew a good place to stay in Edmonton. I said I didn't but that my daughter was meeting me at the station, and she would

Opposite page:
(top) David, grade 11, 1984

(bottom left) David's graduation

(bottom right) Henry and I at David's graduation ceremony, 1985

know. The young man looked so woebegone I asked him if he also needed help finding a place to stay. His English was very limited. All he said was, "Yes please." I found out that his name was Toshiaki Uchibi.

We arrived in Edmonton 48 hours late and Linda, bless her big heart, asked Toshiaki if he would like to come home with us. He said, "Yes please." Can you imagine this boy on his own by himself in a strange country not having a very good command of the language and only a thin plaid shirt and no jacket! He wanted to rent a car and go through the mountains. Well, with Linda's help and one of her jackets, he did just that. We found a friend for life. We wrote for a long time and the following year, he came to Bashaw and visited me for two days. Toshiaki told me he envied my home and all my friends. A lonely fellow, I think.

Around the time I got back from Toronto, Ida was in the Millwoods hospital and was diagnosed with colitis. Not a good scene. I looked after Megan for awhile.

David

David still had a year of high school left, so he stayed on at the house in Nisku with Cathy and the kids. I remember him saying, "Mom, this isn't the way things are done. It's usually the *kids* that leave home, not the parents." David did his high school at Wagner Composite in Edmonton, where he did very well. He was in a music program and a teacher brought out David's musical talent.

David married Lori Scott and they now live in Fairview with their three children, Savannah, Stephanie and Shaelynn. David got his ticket in carpentry and he has his own trailer building business. Before that, he was a painter on an off-shore oilrig on the Beaufort Sea. That was a real highlight for him. David and Lori built their own house, which was quite an experience for them. Lori has been good for David. She is a wonderful

"I remember Mom getting off the train with this young, terrified-looking Japanese man. When I got up to them, Mom said, "Here's my daughter, she'll help you!" Being my mother's daughter, of course, I took him home with me!"

Linda

"During Toshiaki's visit, he took my family and me out to a Japanese restaurant. Till then, he hadn't spoken much because his English was limited. As soon as we got to the restaurant, he started talking to the staff in Japanese. My youngest son Keegan blurted out, "He can speak! Toshiaki can speak!"

Linda

"I really enjoyed the music program in high school. There, I learned to compose, record, perform and play in a group environment, all things I still do and enjoy today."

David

"The first time I met David's mom I was so nervous, being only 19 at the time, and probably feeling very self-conscious to boot. I kind of knew right then and there that we would get along just fine. I have so appreciated her gentleness, the way she sits and ponders her thoughts before speaking (a gift I would love to learn), but mostly her acceptance of who you are as a person. And I love her dearly for that."

Lori, Mary's daughter-in-law

"I used to be quite certain that it would be impossible for anyone to get lost in Fairview. Well, then Mom came to town!

David

mother who is very personable and is a wonderful addition to our family. Like my girls, David has grown up to be a very responsible person.

On one trip I made to Fairview, David was playing keyboard in a band for a Hawaiian dance. It was a lot of fun. I was so proud and excited to see David playing and singing in a band. It made me so happy that he had this accomplishment. It does a mother's heart good. David now plays the organ in his church for sing-songs.

After the Hawaiian dance, I got lost trying to find David and Lori's place. I was an hour fishing my way around Fairview. Finally, I went to the police station and they got me to David and Lori's place. When I got there, I dropped my keys in a snowbank. The police probably thought I was drinking! What a drag! It was 3:00 a.m. Lori was sleeping and I came in the door the same time as David.

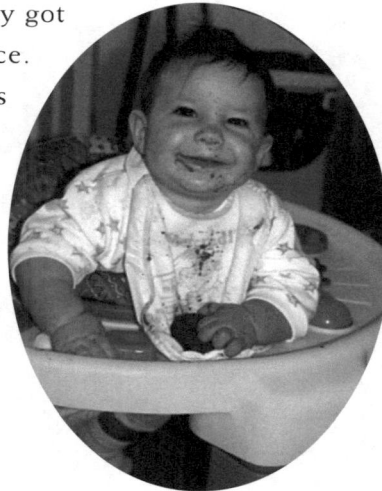

"When she comes to visit, I wish she could stay forever."

Granddaughter Stephanie, seven

"Granny deBoon is a very caring grandmother. She cares more about others than herself, and she has grandchildren that love her more than anything in the world."

Granddaughter Savannah, nine

"Ga, ga."

Granddaughter Shaelynn, 15 months.

Opposite page:
(top left) The eve of David's wedding, 1986

(top right) David and Lori's wedding, 1986

(bottom left) David and Lori, 1998

(bottom right) David playing in a band on New Year's Eve, mid-1990s

This page:
(top) Stephanie (age 6) and Savannah (age 8)

(bottom) Shaelynn (9 months)

7

My Dream Home and a New Community: Bashaw — 1984-1997

Henry and I decided to name our place Monarch Acres. How this came about is, when we were driving to Bashaw from Ponoka in August of 1983, there was a huge migration of monarch butterflies. There were so many butterflies that they were hitting the windshield and landing on the hot road. I said, "Look at that, the butterflies are migrating and so are we." I had a fellow from a farmers' market make us a name plate that said, "Henry and Mary, Monarch Acres." To me, butterflies represent freedom of the spirit and resurrection of life.

The house in Bashaw was just lovely. In addition to all the usual things, it had a large open-concept living room, a large fireplace, two regular bathrooms, and a half bath off the master bedroom. There were three bedrooms upstairs and room to sleep four to six people in the basement. The stonework for the fireplace covered an entire wall in the living room. A huge house for two people but my kids sure liked it when they came to visit. Moving to Bashaw was a big adjustment for me, as I left my family up North. For three months I didn't know anyone. I guess no one in the town knew that we had moved there. Finally in the fall the neighbour women phoned and asked if I would like to go bowling in Stettler. After that I went with a bunch every week.

I put in a large garden and since there was no landscaping done, I proceeded to establish flower beds. I bought bags of dirt but mostly I made the flower beds from molehill dirt. Every day, I would go out with two ice cream pails and fill them with dirt from molehills. The reason I did this is because the regular soil was so

"I was glad to see her in that glory-home on the hill. It was something she very much deserved. Living in Bashaw enabled her to share all of the talents that she has with regards to people and organizing."

Cathy

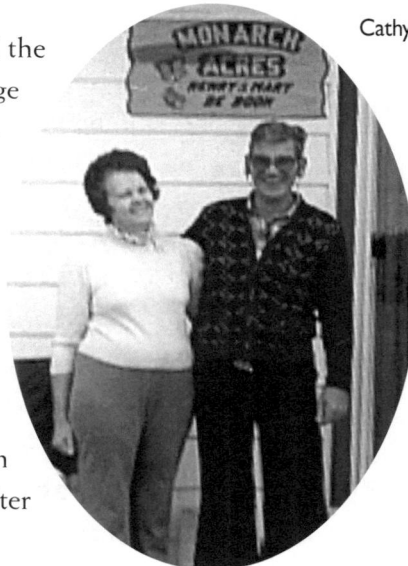

Opposite page:
Our dream home in Bashaw

"I remember eating peas with Granny when we were picking them. We kept stopping for pea breaks."

Grandson Mathew, 17

"I remember jumping off the shed roof into the snow."

Jordan, seven

Opposite page:

1. Ellen won the arm-wrestling match!

2. Cathy and me

3. Ida and opponent

4. I won! Linda is beside me.

5. Bowling champs of the Senior Winter Games, 1985

6. Henry (closest) and David (furthest), with Rob watching

7. Rob and Ida

8. David and Lori

9. Linda and Cathy

This page:

(top) I used to saw wood for our fuel-efficient wood-burning stove.

(middle) Henry and I singing a song together for one of our Christmas gatherings

(bottom) Playing the spoons at a Christmas gathering at Cathy and Bernie's

poor and molehill dirt is the best. Finally I had some very nice flower beds. I always said I was building a mountain out of a molehill!

I started bowling in Stettler and going to the local senior's centre in Bashaw (The Happy Gang Centre), which made me very happy. And Henry, my, how happy he was in Bashaw. He was a man who hardly ever played, but loved to work. Henry arranged to have a new well put in and also a natural gas line. He also fibreglassed the deck on the porch. He kept the weeds down and spent many Saturdays burning the weeds in the ditches. Boy, did he ever have some huge fires going. I recall it was a black winter in '85 so David and Henry decided to burn some very high weeds south of the house. There was a strong wind so the flames must have been high as our house. I should say here, we later put all our carrots and potatoes down the new well-site to keep them fresh through the winter.

One thing I really enjoyed in Bashaw was being able to go biking when the weather permitted. Many times, I encountered deer and beaver. There are a lot of ponds and rolling hills around Bashaw. I remember one spring, early in the morning, coming across a family of geese: two sets of parents and 22 goslings. They were sunning themselves on the road and then they very slowly and quietly slipped into the pond. I remember another time in the fall when a flock of swans flew over. That was something to see. In the evening, I could hear the owls calling. I have always loved nature so all these experiences were like food for the soul.

Another thing I loved about Bashaw was the family events that we could have in such a big house. Early on, we held a number of variety shows and Christmas concerts. One time Bob and his new family came, and Ken and Mary (Frankie), and Mr. And Mrs. Portlock (Peter's parents). That was a full house! Most people did skits or sang songs, while others watched. We had a ball. There was always plenty of room for the grandchildren to play in the basement and outside in the yard.

Country Fair and Winter Games

I think it was that first summer in Bashaw that the whole family came down for the Bashaw country fair. For a joke, Ellen signed everybody up for all these different contests. Next thing you know, our names are being called out over the loudspeaker getting us to come for these contests of arm wrestling, log sawing and nail pounding. Well, that turned out to be some fun. Ellen won the arm wrestling in her weight group and I won the nail pounding in my age category! I used to go to those fairs all the time, winning prizes for my flowers, canning, vegetable growing and embroidery.

In the winter of '85, from February 28 to March 2, I went with a few others to the Senior Winter Games in Edson. This fellow from Stettler and myself won a gold medal for Alberta in the high and low bowling. It was some fun. When I got back to bowling at Stettler, just for fun, whoever scored highest got to wear my gold medal for awhile.

1

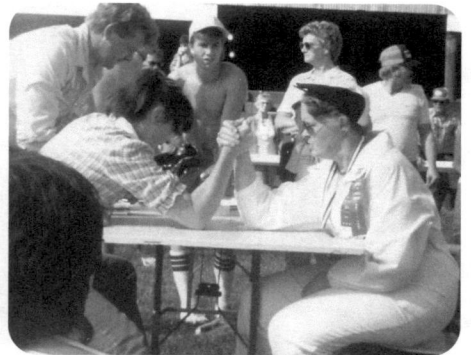
2

3

4

5

6

7

8

9

Starting to Paint

In 1985, I joined art classes and I really enjoyed painting. My daughter Cathy and two of my sisters also paint.

Excerpt of a Mother's Day Card From Ellen, 1985

I found this Mother's Day card last January, while I was still in shock over seeing your incredible paintings. You are truly an artist. But then I got to thinking, I should not be so shocked because you have been a true artist ever since I can remember:

You painted me a happy childhood, the colours of which are still with me. You always saw some goodness in the badness all around. From scratch you created a good outlook on life. Those around you have been your canvas; your words and your ways have been your paints.

So you see, it's not so shocking, this talent you have found. It is just the physical manifestation of your inner beauty that has been there all along.

There are no words to express how grateful I am that you are my Mom. Happy Mother's Day.

Love,
Ellen Rose

This page:

(top) I started painting at age 57.

(middle) I displayed my paintings in many Bashaw art shows.

(bottom left) Cathy has painted and sold hundreds of pictures.

(bottom right) Cathy presented Ralph Klein, the provincial premier, with a limited edition print of Leduc's first oil well.

Henry Breaks a Leg

On November 9, 1986, Henry was late coming home from Meeting Creek and he fell down the incline coming out of the shop. He lay on the ground about 10 minutes then he realized, "I can't lie here; I will die." It was bitterly cold and starting to snow, so he pulled himself over the ground to the truck, which was a good 50 feet away. He tried to start the truck and couldn't because of his cold hands. He kept waving at people driving by, but they thought he was just being friendly and they kept driving. He was in the cold truck about an hour. Finally, he decided to try to get back in the shop where it was warm. He got out on the ground, and started pulling himself along. David, the shop foreman came along, wondering why the lights were still on and why Henry's truck was still there on a Friday night.

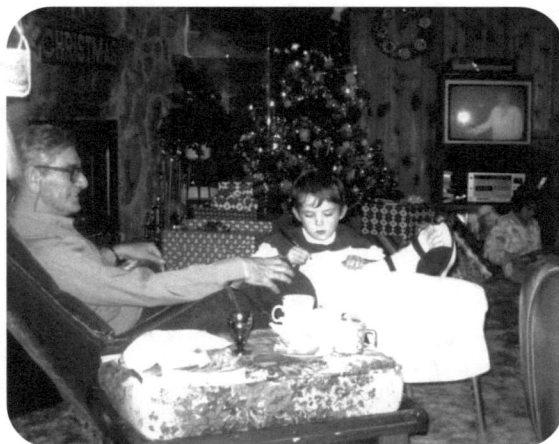

As quickly as possible, David got Henry to the Bashaw hospital. They cut his pants off, and the rest of his clothes, and wrapped him in warm blankets. He broke the two long bones in his right leg in two places. The bones were sticking out at one place. I was called, and after they gave him a shot of Demerol for the pain, we drove very fast to Edmonton by ambulance. I will never forget that trip because we drove into a full-blown blizzard. I phoned Peter and Linda and they came over immediately. They were so supportive and I stayed about 10 days with them.

All that winter, Henry's leg was not very good and the following June, when the cast was taken off, they found out the leg did not set. This time he had a pin put in from knee to ankle. To make a long story short, he was another nine months on crutches and, later, a walking cast.

The Happy Gang Centre

During this same year, I was elected president of the Golden Age Club, better known as the Happy Gang Centre. It was a place where seniors could go for a social time. We had shuffleboard, pool, cards and darts. I would go out in the afternoon while Henry was at the fibreglass plant in Meeting Creek. It was a challenge but, in spite of different elderly personalities to grapple with, I managed, for the most, to enjoy my position. I think my sense of humour got me through a lot of tight situations.

During my time there, I started Friendship Days. Once a month we had sing-songs

"She was a wonderful president. She fitted in so nice. We just loved her. She could take over and entertain us so. She made such a happy atmosphere to cheer people up and make people feel welcome. She has a way that makes people feel comfortable. People trusted her."

Madeline Goodwin, member of the Happy Gang Centre, 92

"She made a video night for people who lived alone. She picked people up and gave them rides. She was always organizing things. She's a kind person and always ready to help."

Yvonne De Cnodder, member of the Happy Gang Centre

This page:

(top) Mathew signing Henry's cast.

(bottom) I was the "Young-timer Mascot" for the Happy Gang Centre in the Bashaw parade.

Opposite page:

(top) Ribbon cutting for our new addition

(middle) Our tourist information booth received many awards.

(bottom) Madeline's 90th birthday with Bashaw's mayor and a local MP

This page:

(top) Henry drove the truck that pulled the float for the Happy Gang Centre. The little child is Mathew.

(middle) One day for a surprise, I dressed up as a bag lady and put on a skit.

(bottom) The Happy Gang ladies dressed up for Klondike Days, in 1986

and on special holidays like Valentine's, Halloween and Christmas we decorated the room and dressed up. One time, we did a Hawaiian night. We always had a lot of fun at these functions with our homegrown entertainment. Our Christmas events were well attended. The seniors would portray the Nativity scene. It was a hoot seeing the old men with bath towels on their heads! One time when I was emceeing, the three wise men didn't come out when I said their cue. I said over and over, "And the three wise men came from the East." Well, the three wise men were making so much noise, I finally had to go backstage and practically drag them to the front.

Another time, around Easter, we had a spring fashion show, where the women modelled hats that we made. We were quite surprised when one of the men showed up with a lamp shade on his head. The men in the audience voted for who should get first prize. I won, but I still think the man with the lampshade (Bob Warren) should have won! One night, we had a show where we modelled clothes from the local thrift shop. I dressed up as a bag lady and did a skit about the bag lady who lived in the back streets of Bashaw. I made sausage links from nylon hose and pretended to eat them from a garbage can. I kept sprinkling them with Pepto Bismol, which got a lot of laughs.

I was president for three years, and then after a two-year break, they put me back in for another three years. During my presidency, we went through the growing pains of having a new addition put on the building. I will not go into detail about the growing pains but there were many! One of our members was a retired contractor and he helped us realize our dream. We had our grand opening for that on June 18, 1991. The ribbon was cut and we had a lovely program. One special part was when we sprinkled water from the River Jordan on the doorways of the new addition. Ellen had brought this water back, in a small shampoo bottle, from the Holy Land where she travelled as

a teenager. After the water was sprinkled, the building was blessed by four ministers and a lovely lunch was served.

Our seniors' club was responsible for running the Bashaw tourist information booth. The $3000 we made from that helped with the upkeep of our seniors' centre. Over the years, we were presented with many efficiency awards for all around good service to the people who came for information.

Before my time as president, my friend Madeline Goodwin was president for 12 years. I always enjoy telling a good joke wherever an opening presents itself and I remember Madeline telling me a good one called The Story of the Bees: This is the story of a little bee whose sex is very hard to see. You cannot tell the he from the she. The busy bee is never still. She has no time to take the pill. That is why in times like these, there are so many sons of bees! I told this joke at Madeline's 90th birthday party, which was held at the Happy Gang Centre, as were many other birthday and anniversary parties. The Centre plays an important role in the lives of seniors in Bashaw.

After my presidency with the Happy Gang Centre, I became the president of the hospital auxiliary.

"I remember the Happy Gang Centre. One time, I went running in there and got in trouble for wearing my shoes on the new floor-curling place!"

Grandson Mathew, 17

"She's a beautiful woman. I love her like a sister. I didn't have a real sister—my sister died when I was three. But I couldn't have had a better one when I got older. I love that woman."

Madeline Goodwin, 92

"This elderly couple died within an hour of one another and when they got to the Pearly Gates, the woman exclaimed; "What a beautiful place." "Yes" the man replied. "And if hadn't been for you and that darn oat bran we would have been here sooner."

Mary in a letter to Ellen, 1998.

Excerpt From Letter to Ellen in 1997

I have to tell you something neat I am doing. There is a woman in town here and she's 92 or 93. Since I moved here she lost all her children in a terrible car accident. I think there were five in the accident. Anyway, I have decided to make myself her secret friend or pal, if you like. I made up a poem that rhymed and got the florist to deliver a bunch of flowers to her. The poem said you will find out who your secret pal is next Valentines' Day. (Maybe she won't be alive by then. A chance I have to take. But who knows? She still drives her own car.) Now for all the special occasions in the year, I will make up a poem and send it to her. Hopefully she won't guess who it is.

"Mom was always looking out for other people. I remember her making sure that neighbours who were down on their luck got a special hamper of food and gifts at Christmas. She would often befriend children who needed a bit of extra love. Our home was always open to strangers. She would often say, "Sure they can come, we'll just throw another spud in the pot."

Ellen

The Blizzard of 1988

You know it's funny, when a person starts recalling events, the dramatic, traumatic, even the horrific always come to the forefront. I suppose this is because the events leave a lasting impression in one's memory. I remember on July 31 of '87, a tornado hit Edmonton, destroying homes and businesses and killing several people. In 1988, I saw the worst blizzard I've ever seen in my lifetime.

On the evening of March 27, 1988, the proverbial March lion came roaring in from the north. Funny thing, the weatherman missed predicting this storm so no one was prepared. Even the highways were full of travellers. Well, everything came to a standstill. There were six-feet drifts all around the house. In fact, they were eight feet in the back of the house. I owned a video camera at the time, so I would open the south side patio doors and take a picture every two hours. I shot the same view – our van and a six-foot spruce tree. Finally, all you could see was six inches of the tree and a few inches of the van's aerial. It was just like the Good Lord had dumped a dollop of ice cream over the van. To top things off, the power went off for a few hours. We weren't too worried, as we had an energy-efficient wood stove in the basement. We stayed downstairs and made soup and coffee on top of the stove.

We had put our snow shovel away in our outside garage so we couldn't get it. Henry, being very innovative, made a push-type shovel out of wood and got the snow off the porch. Finally, he managed, by hanging on to trees, to work his way to the garage for our shovel.

The town of Mirror was without power for two days. They were taking seniors to a local centre by snowmobiles. There were helicopters coming, trying to free cattle caught in the snow. Many cattle died, as the snow was two-and-a-half feet on the level and there were big drifts around as well. They called a state of emergency in Airdrie, north of Calgary. But I really feel, from what I can gather, that the snowfall was much worse in Bashaw.

I had previously planned to have Mathew and Ria-Mae on the Sunday. I phoned Cathy and said there was no way. She said, "But Mom, I need a babysitter bad. Can't the kids just walk in from the road?"

"Cathy," I said, "you can't come. You have to see this to believe it!" You see, they didn't have this storm in the Edmonton area and didn't have a clue it was so bad.

Mathew was so disappointed. He said, "Granny, can't we come? God told me it would be all right." Anyway, they came on Monday.

In the meantime, four men came with a big front-end loader and a smaller tractor with a blade. You know, the most wonderful thing about this was we hadn't even

phoned anyone to plough us out. They just came. In fact, Mel Hay of Bashaw was on the big tractor and he wouldn't even take any money for his trouble. He made a mountain of snow at the back about 11 feet tall. Ria-Mae and Mathew had a lot of fun playing on top of this mound of snow. By Tuesday, the sun came out, and the temperature rose to 60° (Fahrenheit) so then there was water running everywhere!

And do you know, Linda and Ida went on a camping trip to Waterton Lake that weekend. I was worried about them and thought they were nuts. Anyway the storm didn't come their way.

Henry and I Turn 60

The year of 1988 was momentous. Henry and I both turned 60. My family is great for surprises so on Sunday around 2:00 p.m., David, Lori, Cathy and the kids called Henry and me downstairs and there was Peter and Linda and their new family! Peter and Linda were in the process of adopting three native brothers— Keegan, three-and-a half; Joshua (Peter Jr.), four-and-a-half; and Travis (John), eight-and-a-half. What a wonderful surprise— three handsome boys! I remember one time when Henry and I took Ria-Mae, Mathew, Keegan, Peter Jr., and John on a steam-train tour ride from Stettler. It was quite an experience. The kids were so lively I was afraid they would fall off the train.

Anyway, getting back to the day of the party, after the gang in the basement sang "Happy Birthday" to us, we all tramped upstairs. There was a huge cardboard box sitting in the middle of the living room floor. Someone said, "Mom, come over here and open this box— it's a special delivery from Toronto." The box was marked, "Fragile, handle with care." I opened the box and out popped Ellen, complete with a red bow in her hair. Well, I never suspected a thing! It floored me and I had to sit down for a long time. Henry was warned about this, as the kids were worried it would be too much of a shock for his heart.

It was a truly lovely experience. About 20 people came from Bashaw. Ellen was home for about a week, which I enjoyed. The party was for our birthdays but it was also a bon voyage send-off because we were getting ready to go to Holland on June 11th.

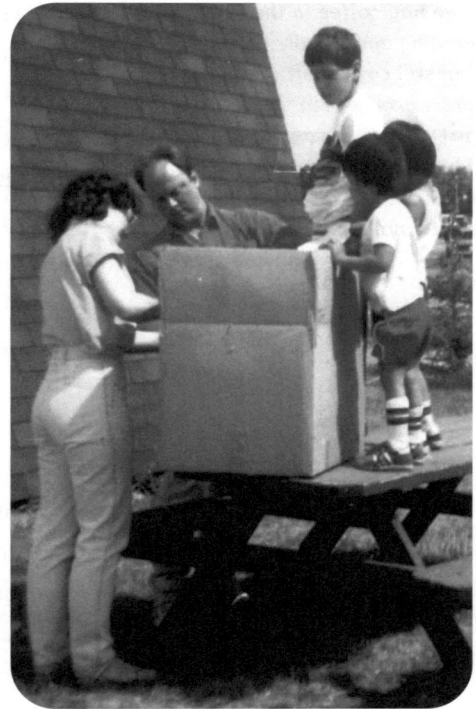

"As fun as it was to surprise Mom, I realized that maybe that was the last time we should startle her like that! I have also come to believe that, sometimes, it's an even bigger gift to let someone anticipate a treat well in advance of getting it."

Ellen

Opposite page:
David (age 23), Ellen (27), Ida (31), Linda (34) and Cathy (37), 1988

This page:
(top) Keegan, Peter Jr. and John helping Ida and Rob prepare a big surprise for their new Granny

(middle & bottom) My family is famous for surprises!

"We had coffee in the evening and usually there was still coffee left over. In the morning, Henry would just warm it up and drink. That surprised me— it doesn't taste anything the next day!"

Conny

Our Trip to Holland

We flew to Holland with some apprehensions: "Will Henry's heart stand the trip?" "Will I be able to keep up with all the walking and stairs involved?" It was indeed a step of faith. We boarded the plane about 7:30 p.m. It was very interesting going over miles of snow and ice and clouds that looked like cotton balls. As we descended in Amsterdam, I was amazed to see the red tiles on the rooftops. We were met by Richard and Conny and three-month-old Brenda. Immediately we went to a place with windmills and took pictures. Richard and Conny lived in a three-floor apartment. Very tiny and with lots of stairs.

Henry had not been back to Holland for 23 years, so it was a cloud-nine experience for him and for me too. Henry and I took a six-day tour up the River Rhine on a ferry boat. We saw many old castles, vineyards, villages and industrial factories. We travelled in the day and put down anchor at night. Different entertainers came in from some of the cities.

One interesting highlight of the trip was visiting the 600-year-old Cathedral Dome in Cologne, Germany. The stained glass windows have to be seen to be appreciated. Awesome.

In Düsseldorf, Germany, Henry and I decided to go exploring. We got proper lost! We couldn't speak the language and couldn't understand the street signs. After about three hours, we finally made our way to the boat, tired and very hungry. While we were there, Düsseldorf was celebrating its 800th year. This makes us Canadians realize how young our country is.

When we got back to Holland, Richard and Conny showed us something new every day. We were on the road all the time. They certainly showed us a great time. Too bad both Henry and I got bronchitis. After about three weeks, I was really ready to go home.

One thing I should make mention of is that, on the first trip to Holland, I went to an outdoor farmers' market where I saw a kitchen band. This inspired me to go back home and start one myself.

The Bashaw Kitchen Band

In September 1988, I put the word out about starting a kitchen band. I asked people to come to my house thinking I would only get about six or so. Well, 17 people showed up! And so began *The Happy Bang Kitchen Band*. We practised about three times and we got asked to play for the Golden Age Club's 20th anniversary. We didn't do too bad for beginners. We got our heads together and came up with costumes of gingham aprons and scarfs, with white blouses and black skirts. The men wore red bow ties to match the red in the women's aprons and scarfs. I asked Laura Pearson to lead and direct the band. So in her, we had a good leader. After she stepped down, I took over. It was a big responsibility, looking for bookings and arranging rides.

Opposite page:

(top) Our kitchen band in Bashaw was a lot of fun!

(bottom pics) When it came to making our own fun, there was no moss growing under our bottoms.

During eight years, we played for nursing homes, birthdays, anniversaries, lodges, Christmas and Mother's Day parties. We played all over, including Red Deer, Ponoka, Rimbey, Camrose and many other places. One time, we played together with the Camrose kitchen band for a spring social of the Happy Gang Centre. What fun. But the most exciting thing was when we went on the TV. The CBC used to have a program called "Alberta Express." They would go around Alberta filming different things and somehow they got a hold of our name. They set up a day to come, and ended up filming for several hours. We got eight minutes on the TV. What an exciting time for all of us and the townspeople. There were 200 people came to watch the filming. At the time, Bashaw only had a population of 875 people. A little bit of glory in our lives, to say the least.

"They had a lot of fun in that Kitchen Band! Oh, they made a good impression!"

Yvonne

A Difficult Subject

In December 1988, my daughter Ellen came home and told me she was in a lesbian relationship. It was a grieving experience for me, lasting a long time. Then because of my love for Ellen, I adjusted to the situation.

I look at it this way: something has caused this in a percentage of our worldly population. Lesbians and gays are still a part of God's creation and are not where they are by choice and should not be judged. Luke 6:37, "Do not judge, and you will not be judged; do not condemn, and you will not be condemned; forgive and you will be forgiven."

A Time of Many Losses

In 1989, I lost my oldest sister Thelma. She was buried in Lethbridge on May 28. Thelma was more of a mother to me than my own mother was able to be. As the oldest, she took a lot of responsibility for me. Three or four days later, I had the misfortune of falling and slipping off the front step of the tourist information booth. It was around seven in the evening and it was pouring rain. No one was about, and I was in a great deal of pain. I picked myself up off the ground and drove myself to the hospital. They took X-rays. Nothing showed up so I went home.

I started therapy on my arm and after a month, they said, "Mary, we can't straighten out your arm. Go back to your doctor." The doctor sent me to a specialist in Red Deer who took more X-rays. They showed that a bone was out of place and my elbow was broke. I was operated on the next morning and a pin was put in. I had a cast from my fingers to my shoulder. The next day, they rushed me out because the Queen of England was coming to view the hospital that day! This was way too early. I ended up developing a blood clot in my leg. What a drag, lying for two weeks with my feet up and my arm hurting. I was in that darned cast for 10 weeks and had therapy for several

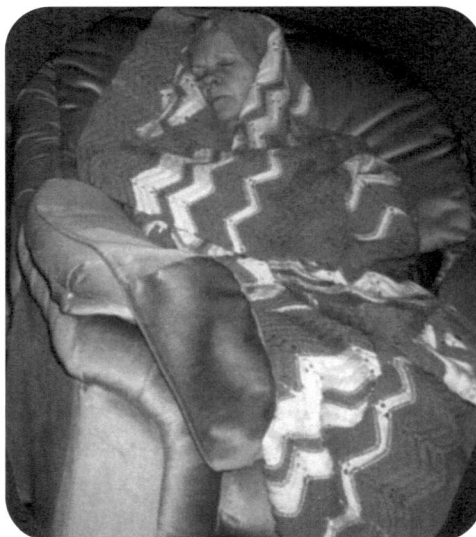

Opposite page: *(top) Henry and I, a few years before he passed away*

(right pics) I often talked about wanting to ride in a hot air balloon.

This page:
(top) My oldest sister, Thelma, in 1981

(bottom) I had to spend a lot of time resting after I broke my arm.

weeks after that. Now, I have to say, my arm finally turned out ok but 1990 was a lost cause.

It got worse when Henry up and had another heart attack. The eighth one in so many years. This one really slowed him down. He couldn't go to work. All he did was jigsaw puzzles. He did go back to work for a bit. Then, on March 1, 1990, Henry passed away while putting wood in the wood burning stove downstairs. He's in a better place now. He was buried at the Heimtal Moravian Church that we used to go to. Cathy designed his tombstone—a picture of a man with a rake and a saying that reads, *Life's Work Well Done*. His mother passed away the year before and his dad, the year before that. Henry was buried on his mother's birthday. I'm glad to say that I still keep in touch with the deBoon family.

It was a big adjustment living alone. So lonely at times. Ida came down and put the garden in that year and I was able to keep the grass cut on the two-and-a-half acres. That year, David came down and built me a beautiful sunroom, which I enjoyed very much. Rob arranged to have an attached garage built for me with an automatic door.

Up, Up and Away!

On my 65th birthday, a party was held at the Happy Gang Centre. My family gave me a ticket for a hot air balloon ride. I always knew there were times my kids wished I would fly away into orbit! It was quite an experience to drift over Edmonton and land in a field north of Beaumont. Ellen was home from Toronto and we went to the mountains for a few days.

Canada to Holland—Holland to Canada

In the mid 1990s, I took another trip to Holland. Richard and Conny sure showed me a good time and I enjoyed seeing their two girls, Brenda and Wendy. The weather was exceptionally good while I was there. We had a lot of fun trying to communicate because the girls couldn't speak English and I couldn't speak much Dutch. We com-

"We borrowed a wheelchair and went racing through Amsterdam. Mary really wet her pants."

Richard

"Wendy and Brenda had fun with "Oma Canada" because her Dutch was so poor. A knife became a spoon and a spoon became a fork. Her Dutch was a hopeless case. We had a lot of fun about that. With the girls, Mary used the word "lekker" a lot; it means "a nice taste."

Richard

"When we went with the two girls to Canada, we tried to prepare them about the food and everything. Brenda is not a good eater, so when I told her the amount of food in restaurants is twice as much as Holland, she started crying and she said she didn't want to go."

Richard

"We were with Oma (Grandma) in a restaurant in Canada, and the girls got chewing gum. Mary took chewing gum also and the three of them decided to make those bubble balls. Mary got such a big one and it broke all over her nose and cheeks. The girls had a really big laugh: "How can a granny do something like that!"

Conny

municated by hugs! One thing that stands out for me about that trip was that they took me to the art gallery in Amsterdam. Richard pushed me in a wheelchair, going like heck over the cobblestones, with me screeching and hollering. Boy, he pushed me around like the dickens!

A while after this trip, Richard, Conny and the girls came to Canada. We rented an RV and took a trip through BC. We had a lot of rain, but we did manage to hit a few sunny spells. When we were driving, Richard, Conny and the kids sang Dutch songs and I hummed along. One afternoon, the girls wanted a snack. I couldn't understand exactly what they wanted so I pulled one thing after another out of the fridge. Both of them would chorus, "Nay! Nay!" until I finally got the right thing— peanut butter!

We had a good time on that trip.

When we got home, my place was overgrown with weeds and my lawn needed mowing. Richard and Conny cut the grass and pulled the weeds and Richard built me a compost. Conny gave the RV a thorough cleaning.

Emerald 25th Anniversary Tour

While living in Bashaw, I took in a few seniors' tours. When I was much younger, there was this popular band called the Emeralds. In 1995, I went on a tour where the Emeralds rode on the tour bus with us, and then entertained us in the evening. I was lined up with a roommate by the name of Elsie Knoske. At the last minute, the company asked us if we would mind going triple occupancy. The third person happened to be a lady from Bashaw, Mary Felt. We boarded a plane in Edmonton, headed for Los Angeles. There, we met two buses. There were 86 people on that tour – 10 widows, and the rest couples. Half the band rode on one bus, and the rest on the other. We got to know them one-on-one. That was nice.

We travelled around Los Angeles on down to San Diego and Tijuana for shopping. Then we stopped for five days in Mesa, Arizona. We went to eight dances in 16 days. This was one of the best tours I was ever on. Mary, Elsie and myself got on very well and found many things to laugh about. For example, once Elsie tried to put on Mary Felt's pants by accident. When she said, "Oh, these aren't mine," I exclaimed, "I thought on this trip that we might get into one another's hair, but I didn't think we'd try and get into one another's pants."

Trip to Maui

In 1994, Linda and Peter invited me to go along with them to Maui. We drove to Spokane where we caught a plane. The swimming and beaches were nice and I really enjoyed snorkelling. I took a thrilling trip by helicopter over the island's volcanoes and lush valleys. In one place, we dipped almost to the base of a very big waterfall and then flew up again. That area gets over 200 inches of rain a year so the growth was large and lush. I got black from the sun and when I got home, people seemed so pale, I thought they looked sick.

"When I think about Mary, she is a remarkable woman filled with love, peace, patience and joy."

Conny

"She is someone who walks with life. She enjoys it!"

Richard

Opposite page:
(top) I had a good time visiting Richard, Conny, Wendy and Brenda in Holland.

(bottom) Brenda, Wendy and I communicated by hugs!

This page:
Linda and I in Maui

"We felt kind of guilty, but it was a joke. The joke was on us!"

Madeline, referring to her accidental trip into a bar.

Madeline's First Trip to a Bar

Here's a story that may tickle your fancy. One Saturday evening, I picked up my friend Madeline Goodwin for supper. We decided to drive to Mirror. The café, called the Whistle Stop, was closed, so what to do? We started to look for the café in the hotel.

When we walked in, a bunch of people we knew walked in before us and we just followed them along. Next thing you know, we were in the bar! We found out the café was closed but that we could get a steak supper in the bar.

Well, did we have fun. There was a lot of good-natured kidding especially of Madeline, who was 90 and it was her first time in a bar, ever. One of the people went all over town trying to find film for his camera. He was going to have a picture put in the Bashaw Star.

The steak supper was very good and the people even treated us. Madeline and I excused ourselves as soon as possible saying we had a card party. We laughed all the way back to Bashaw. We really fell into that one.

On the Move Again

During the spring of 1997, near the end of April, I decided to sell my acreage and move to Camrose, which has 45 per cent retired people. One reason I wanted to move there was because it has so much to offer culturally. So many more activities like swim-

Opposite page:

(top) Nine of my beautiful grandchildren, 1996

(bottom) A peaceful moment: Cathy painted the picture above my head.

This page:

(top) Madeline and I having dinner at Wong's restaurant in Bashaw.

(bottom) My family spent many enjoyable times in my dream home in Bashaw.

ming and singing. Another reason is that the services are better in Camrose. In Bashaw, we no longer had an emergency ward at the hospital and we only had one doctor for the whole town. One time, I needed to go by ambulance to an emergency ward. It scared me because it was a half-hour trip to Camrose. What if it had been a real serious thing? Even though I was less than a mile from Bashaw, I was already a Camrose taxpayer because my property fell within the Camrose county boundary. I found this out the hard way when a grass fire got away from me and I had to pay a $500 bill for calling the fire department in Bashaw. Can you imagine what would have happened if I called the fire department in Camrose!

She's one of my favourite people! She never has a negative thing to say. If she can't say something positive, she doesn't say anything at all. I've learned from her. She has a love for people no matter who they are and she's so down-to-earth with everyone.

Frankie (Mary), Mary's sister-in-law, 72

I went in to Century 21 and was taken around to see a lot of houses. I was very disappointed in what was out there and the money they wanted, wow! On Jordan's birthday, I went up to Leduc and told Ida and Rob my story. Rob said, "Why don't you let me build you a house?" Well, I listed my acreage and in less than three weeks, it was sold. The people let me store my furniture in the Bashaw house because it was such short notice and my house wasn't built yet.

To make a long story short, I stayed four months at Rob and Ida's, while a beautiful house was being built for me in Camrose. I remember thinking how nice it was to be living with a family unit again. I enjoyed helping Ida can high bush cranberries but they smelled like dirty socks! While I was there, I sang in a choir called the Telford Singers, went swimming once a week, rode my bicycle every day and took mouth organ lessons. Also, I was able to spent some quality time with Mary (Frankie, my sister-out-law) who lives in Leduc now.

8

My Last Earthly Move: Camrose — 1997 onward

I moved into the house in Camrose November 2, 1997. It is a lovely home with two bedrooms and an open-style kitchen and dining-room, living-room. A few days later, the movers and I went to Bashaw to get my furniture. Man, before the furniture came, I bet every tradesman there is was running through the house at the last minute. Ida and the wife of my realtor (Kathy) came to help me. I don't ever want to move again. On the following Saturday, I roasted a chicken and Cathy, Bernie and Mathew came over for dinner. They brought me a dozen roses. Lovely. Helga Jacobs from the Welcome Wagon came here with so many gifts from different businesses.

"I wish she still had that big house (in Bashaw) so we could visit her there."

Granddaughter Stephanie, seven

Generally, there's something lovely about Camrose that I like. It's a very picturesque city of 15,000 people. In 1998, Camrose came in second in Western Canada for its beautification ideas. It has a nice lake in the middle and a fountain. They keep swans in this lake. In the winter, they house the swans, and in the summer they let them loose.

Because of El Niño, my first winter in Camrose was open and had only about two weeks of snow and cold. What a beautiful winter. I joined the Cream Puffs, the Camrose kitchen band. For a few months, I hid the fact that I was the leader of the Bashaw kitchen band. But it soon came to light and, before I knew it, I was leading

Opposite page:
Me telling my kids, "Remember to eat your vegatables."

This page:
My beautiful house that Rob built

I come to the garden alone,
while the dew is still on the roses

My mother had a great love of gardening and especially of growing beautiful flowers.

Mom Long took me under her wing and proceeded to teach me how to tend a garden.

I enjoyed farm life. When I was pregnant with my first baby, I had a big garden.

While at Judson, I raised a nice garden.

In Thorsby, we had a big yard where I could grow a big garden.

We were never hungry (in Nisku) with a garden.

I put in a large garden in Bashaw and since there was no landscaping done, I proceeded to establish flower beds.

I made all these centre pieces for the tables at the 25th anniversary party for the (Camrose) senior's drop-in centre. Well, you'd never guess what happened: someone went and swiped the geraniums half an hour before the event. Imagine that! So, I hoped in my van and tore downtown and got some more flowers. You can't have a centre piece without flowers!

Do you know what happened this morning? When I was watering my flowers, I put the garden hose down and, wouldn't you know, the danged thing wasn't off and it went straight up like a fountain and sprayed me all over. I'm standing here all wet!

I sure do like gardening. I guess I got that from Mother.

O the beautiful garden, the garden of pray'r

again. I also joined the Golden Tones, a seniors' choir out of the Camrose Seniors' Centre. I sing alto and enjoy this very much. I also took up swimming exercises. I continue to take seniors' tours. For example, I went to Victoria for two weeks with a tour group of 46 other seniors. When I think of the time when my parents were seniors, it's too bad they didn't have the availability of many of these things. To coin a phrase, "You've come a long way, baby!"

All told, I moved 18 times to get to Camrose. These many moves broadened me more than if I'd lived only in one little puddle. I hope that Camrose is my last earthly move, before I move onto a higher plain!

Opposite page:
The flowers blooming in front of my house, 1999

This page:
(left) My favourite chair is in the right-hand corner of my living room.

(right) Playing my harmonica in the kitchen

Epilogue:
An Emotional Journey

In the summation of my book, it has been a journey of mixed emotions. To write this has been emotional and also to temper all things a bit of humour has been thrown in here and there. When I look back on my life, I think what really helped me was being able to laugh in the face of adversity. During hard times, I fought against giving up or withdrawing into myself and away from society. I think I just always felt there was something better. It's hard for people to know that sometimes while in the struggle. My faith kept me going through the valleys to the peaks. You cannot appreciate the stars that come out at night unless you have the dark behind. At this point in time, I would say that my cup is running over.

I am content that all of my children are doing well in their chosen professions and activities. They are all solid citizens making their own contributions to society. I am extremely proud of them and love them all very much. Years ago, I remember praying that my children would get good partners, and I definitely feel that prayer has been answered. I feel blessed having wonderful grandchildren.

This book has been written for my family, who I love more than life. It is my hope that it will have valued meaning to my children and their children's children and so on. Remember my loved ones, my life has been built on the strong faith of Jesus Christ and I hope you will all find this faith for yourselves some day.

Mary Middleton deBoon
Written in June 1999, age 71

My Mother's Piano

Written by my sister, Francis

Mother and Dad were both very musical. Mother had been trained to sing when she was in England. Her father sang in an Anglican church choir for 15 years before he was married. Dad sang in a boys' choir, played the accordion and the mouth organ by ear. He used to sit in the yard of the homestead and play. The horses would come around and put their snouts over his shoulder. They liked the music too.

Tom and Ellen (Nellie) Middleton wanted their children to have a musical education, but times were very hard, and money was scarce in those days. They heard of a piano that was for sale by a Caplee Fanning. He had bought it from a Mrs. Charlie Folk. She inherited it from her folks and took lessons on it when she was a little girl. Caplee Fanning heard my folks wanted a piano, and he asked $150 for it. Nellie did not know how she could help Tom raise that much money, as it was a lot in those days. However, she got the janitor job at the Burwash school for $7 a month. With this work, as well as with raising a few pigs, they finally had enough money to buy that beautiful piano.

I used to go with her sometimes to the school which was an eighth of a mile from the homestead. It was very, very cold. Some mornings it was -25° to -30° (Fahrenheit). Mother put the fire on in the furnace in the small, dugout basement under the one-room school house. Sometimes it was hard to get it going. Then she went upstairs and tidied the school. After school hours she went back again and swept the school out. Sometimes it was very dirty and muddy. Thelma and I went with her. Poor wee thing, so frail and not ever too strong.

Then came the day when the piano was moved into the homestead house. It was a beautiful piano with a lovely tone. Now, to look for a music teacher for Thelma and me. It was an unheard thing to give a boy music lessons even though Walter was perhaps the most musical of all of us. My mother found a stone-deaf lady, Mrs. Fred Gardiner, who could teach us. She lived five miles from us. We had an old horse called Jack and every Saturday afternoon we climbed on the old horse's back and rode bareback to our music lessons. The deaf lady was a marvellous teacher. She charged 50 cents a lesson. It was not long until both Thelma and I were playing that piano real well. Eventually my Dad bought the Gardiner farm and we moved there. I never forgot how beautiful Mrs. Gardiner played the piano. One selection I remember her playing was Three O'clock in the Morning.

We continued taking lessons from a Mrs. Howell, the postmaster's wife. I won first prize for being the best pupil. I won a wonderful music book called the Giant King, which I still have. I took Toronto Conservatory exams up to grade four, then I just continued taking lessons. But Thelma, being better at music, continued and taught her sister Edna lessons. Thelma took lessons from a Mrs. Atzinger and obtained a teacher's certificate. She became a music teacher and taught lessons for several years in Ironsprings and Picture Butte.

Ellen also took a few lessons herself, also little Mary was ready for a few lessons. Ellen learned very fast, but Mary did not practice very much.

Family Births and Deaths

Mary's Parents

Thomas Alfred Middleton, 1883-1956 (immigrated to Canada by ship in 1904)
> Born of Frances Harriet Middleton (née Pays, born in France) and
> Joseph Daniel Middleton (born in Ilkitson, near London, England)

Ellen Middleton (née Scott), 1888-1970 (immigrated to Canada by ship in 1910)
> Born of Elizabeth Ann Scott (née Snowdon) and
> William Turner Scott

Me, Edna, Walter, Thelma, Francis, early 1980s

Mary's Sisters and Brother

Thelma Elizabeth Middleton, 1911-1989, m. Emil Rieter
Ellen Francis Middleton, b. December 17, 1912, m. Roy Burns
Walter Thomas Middleton, b. August 26, 1915, m. Mabel Johnston
Edna Grace Middleton, b. July 18, 1917, m. Wilfred Warren

Mary and Family

Mary Victoria Middleton deBoon, b. June 3, 1928
> m. Bobbie (Bob) Norris Long, b. March 18,1926, d. January 21, 1999
> m. Henry deBoon, b. June 10, 1928, d. March 1 1990

Melvin Douglas Long, b. June 21,1950, d. July 22, 1950

Catherine Anne Long, b. September 14, 1951 m. Bernard (Bernie) Kowalewski,
> b. June 25, 1954

Ria-Mae Long, b. May 9, 1979, m. Scott Cranston, 1973
Mathew Dayson Long, b. September 23, 1981
Darren Rice, b. December 18, 1971 or 1972
> (Last known address #2 Killynure Park, Carryduff, Belfast,
> Northern Ireland, BT8 8PS)

Linda Lorraine Long, b. April 30, 1954 m. Peter John Portlock, b. December 24, 1946
John Travis Long Portlock, b. December 4, 1979
Peter Joshua Long Portlock, b. October 14, 1983
Keegan Long Portlock, b. November 12, 1984

Ida Marie Long, b. September 10, 1957 m. Rob Howe, b. June 2, 1955
Megan Stephanie Howe, b. October 16, 1989
Jordan Robert Howe, b. May 18, 1992

Ellen Rose Long, b. June 18, 1961 partner, **Eve Goldberg**, b. August 11, 1967

David Tracy Long, b. October 17, 1965 m. Lorelei Scott, b. August 13, 1966
Savannah Lei Long, b. January 10, 1990
Stephanie Mary Long, b. October 30, 1991
Shaelynn Michelina Long, b. February 28, 1998

Richard John deBoon, b. March 6, 1959 m. Conny deBoon, b. April 3, 1960
Brenda Jacoba deBoon, b. February 19, 1988
Wendy Johanne deBoon, b. October 9, 1989

With my kids and Bob and his wife, Rose, at a Christmas gathering, mid-1990s

Recipe for Fruit Ambrosia

Fruit Ambrosia

Makes one large bowl
If there's more coming, make more

I make this for special occasions like Christmas and Thanksgiving.
It's a big hit!

2 eggs
⅓ cup lemon juice
½ cup half-and-half cream
1 cup seedless grapes (red or green), halved
1 cup fresh strawberries, sliced
1 tin canned mandarin oranges, drained
1 small can fruit cocktail, drained
1 sliced banana
half-pint container of whipping cream
one package miniature marshmallows
2 tbsp. slivered almonds

Whip the eggs and add the lemon juice and cream. Mix and boil for five minutes, stirring all the while. Turn off heat and let the mixture cool.

Combine the fruit and add the cooled sauce. Mix and put in the fridge overnight.

Shortly before your meal, make the whipping cream. Add the marshmallows and the almonds. Mix with the fruit and enjoy!

Author's Biography

Mary deBoon (née Middleton, formerly Long) is the daughter of Alberta homesteaders. She was educated and is highly skilled in the arts of growing, preparing and preserving her own food, making clothing, engaging everyone around her in home-grown entertainment, and "hanging on" and "making do" in challenging situations. She successfully raised five children, ran two family businesses, and is a well-regarded community leader. Mary has lived in a dozen small Albterta towns and she currently resides in Camrose, where she can be seen touring around town on her scooter, photographing nature scenes.